Winning for Life

Making Every Day, Rich in Every Way

DENIS WAITLEY

Published and distributed by:
SOUND WISDOM
P.O. Box 310
Shippensburg, PA 17257-0310
717-530-2122

info@soundwisdom.com

www.soundwisdom.com

While efforts have been made to verify information contained in this publication, neither the author nor the publisher assumes any responsibility for errors, inaccuracies, or omissions. While this publication is chock-full of useful, practical information; it is not intended to be legal or accounting advice. All readers are advised to seek competent lawyers and accountants to follow laws and regulations that may apply to specific situations. The reader of this publication assumes responsibility for the use of the information. The author and publisher assume no responsibility or liability whatsoever on the behalf of the reader of this publication.

ISBN 13 TP: 978-1-64095-567-7

ISBN 13 eBook: 978-1-64095-568-4

For Worldwide Distribution, Printed in the U.S.A.

1 2 3 4 5 6 7 8 / 28 27 26 25 24

Contents

There are no guaranteed
outcomes in life, only opportunities
disguised as challenges.

Winning is a feeling you
have no ceiling.

Introduction

Welcome to *Winning for Life*. When I created the original *Psychology of Winning* audio album and book, I had no idea it would become one of the most-listened-to programs in the world on personal mastery.

I've had the opportunity to study and inspire winners in every field from Fortune 500 top executives to young entrepreneurs, from NASA astronauts to Olympic athletes and Superbowl champions. As former chairman of psychology on the U.S. Olympic Committee's Sports Medicine Council, I've been responsible for the performance enhancement of all American Olympians.

I also am the author of 16 non-fiction books, including several global best sellers, *Seeds of Greatness*, *Being the Best*, and *The Winner's Edge*. I'm probably best known for having sold over 20 million audio programs in 14 languages. But I'll never forget my struggle to break out of an impoverished, scarcity mindset into an abundance mentality and enriched, joyful lifestyle.

I grew up in a low-income, wartime environment, during World War II and the Korean War. While my father was away on the battlefront, my mother worked in a factory. My parents then divorced, and I felt inadequate and mediocre, at best. Believing we would always be at war, I graduated from the U.S. Naval Academy and pursued a career as a naval aviator.

Deep inside, I wanted to help people grow, rather than remain a warrior. I left the navy and plunged into a 10-year self-discovery program learning from some of the world's greatest thought leaders. The results were incredible. Soon I became a colleague and friend of W. Clement Stone, Earl Nightingale, Billy Graham, Dr. Jonas Salk, and Norman Vincent Peale; and later Zig Ziglar, Wayne Dyer, Jim Rohn, John Maxwell, and Stephen Covey. The most amazing part of my journey has been that most authors write their best works about their own success. However, I wrote *The Psychology of Winning* while I was losing. I wrote it to remind myself what I needed to do, to change from loser to winner.

We live in a fast-forward world with more changes in one of our days than in a decade of our grandparents' lives. Every five minutes a new scientific research study is published, involving some new technological or bio-technology discovery. Unfortunately, some of our most incredible technology wonders, including television, the Internet, amazing graphic motion pictures, virtual reality, miniature communication devices, and instant networking bombard our senses 24/7. The average brain has around 50,000 thoughts per day and 70 percent of them are believed to be negative.

Hollywood movie and TV producers are paid well to know what sells. They know that the need to be shocked or titillated is greater than the need to be informed or inspired. The same psychology is what makes a crowd gather at a fight, fire, explosion, or accident. And neuroscience is in full swing on Madison Avenue. Slick, emotional repetitions flow in and the message is powerful. That message says material goods and leisure activities are the only significant sources of happiness. First, they magnify global problems to frighten us. Then, we are led to believe that all of life's problems can be solved by products or services in about sixty seconds, which is why we have become a skin-deep, immediate gratification society. Fashion does not imitate real life. Life imitates fashion.

The media—siding with corporate, political, and ideological pundits—shapes our patterns of eating, sleeping, dressing, and recreation. They help form our values, morals, professional goals, social behavior, and perceptions of the real world. Unfortunately, too many of us exist on a diet of mental "junk food." Not only is it addictive but it also seems to produce an insatiable hunger for more, which leads to emotional malnutrition. The nutrition industry cautions us that we are what we eat. We also become that to which we are most exposed, which means we are what we watch, listen to, and read.

There are as many theories about the media blitz and learning as there are learners, but one thought is clear: We learn by observation, imitation, and repetition. We seize upon role models, observe their actions, imitate—then become what we see, hear, read, feel, and touch. No single realization is as important as this in understanding and dealing with your brain and mind. You can't concentrate on the reverse of an idea. A fear is a goal going in the wrong direction. Your brain can't distinguish real experience from vivid, repeated, emotion-laced images. I believe we have reached a critical tipping point in human development. We are fast becoming what I refer to as "moist robots"—fleshy, feely-touchy, emotional beings functioning in a virtual world, faithfully and often mindlessly carrying out the instructions of hypnotic purveyors of propaganda and quick fixes.

Fortunately, there is a bright side to this scenario. Social media and advanced communication technologies also give us the instant, real-time network to share opinions, enhance diversity, and gain more inclusion, rather than exclusion, of those who live in cultures who believe and view life differently than we do. It's possible that authentic cornerstones for living successfully, which transcend all borders and prejudices, can go viral and permeate the consciousness of succeeding generations. In our virtual work lives and geographically challenged personal relationships, technology helps us stay connected with loved ones and friends, work teams, peers, and colleagues who we, otherwise, would not have an opportunity to see face to face.

The big question is: To whom have you given authority to train your brain? Your early environment? The news or entertainment media? Career politicians? Celebrities? Friends and peers? Tweets, texts, and Instagrams? Isn't it time to take control of your own future and train your brain and make winning your new habit? The answer is a resounding *yes!*

That's why I'm so excited to share with you what I have learned during the past 50 years by trial and error and by studying the attitudes and actions of authentic, enduring champions in their professional and personal lives. In an easy-to-internalize format, this book concentrates on how to lead yourself and others to more effective relationships, to gain increased focus, a healthier, more optimistic view of the future, and how to handle setbacks and challenges with resiliency and emotional intelligence. We also will introduce new research on how to rewire and train your brain like an internal GPS system to reach your goals.

This is for you if you're already highly successful and want to keep the winning edge, if you're dedicated to moving up to the next level, or if you're like me and want to completely transform your life into one of abundance, true wealth, and joy. I hope you're going to relish and benefit from what you're about to experience: Timeless wisdom and timely neuroscience.

It is not what you have done in the past that makes you successful and happy. It is what you are continuing to do with what you have experienced and are continuing to learn. Wealth means nothing without health. Leaving values in your children is more priceless than leaving them valuables in your estate.

Happiness cannot be traveled to, owned, earned, worn, or consumed. Happiness is the spiritual experience of living every minute with love, grace, and gratitude. Time can only be spent, not saved. The secret is making every day rich in every way!

Happiness cannot be traveled to, owned, earned, worn, or consumed. Happiness is the spiritual experience of living every minute with love, grace and gratitude.

Chapter 1

Behind the Mirror:
Breaking Invisible Barriers

SEEING IS BELIEVING, OR IS IT?

When your eyes are open, you see the world that lies outside yourself. You see the items of the room you're in, the people, and the view of the landscape through the window. You take for granted that the objects are real and separate from yourself. However, successful individuals see the act of achieving in advance—vivid, multidimensional, clear. Champions know that "What you see is who you'll be." When you close your eyes, images and thoughts flow through your mind. You may review memories of past events or pre-view future possibilities. You can daydream about what may be or what might have been, and your imagination will take you beyond the limits of space and time. Most people attach little importance to these inner visions. They may seem pleasantly irrelevant, or uncomfortably at odds with the accepted external reality. If you're like most people, you grew up with the idea that "Seeing is believing." In other words, you need to physically see something with your own eyes to believe that it's real. I know many successful individuals who live this way.

But there's an attitude that suggests, "Before you can see it, you have to believe it." This premise holds that our belief system is so powerful that thoughts can actually cause things to happen in the physical world. I also know many successful individuals who live according to this notion of reality. So which concept is nearer the truth? Do you have to see it before you believe it, or believe before you can see it? The answer is: both are basically true. If you can see something in your mind's eye, and you imagine it over and over again, you will begin to believe it is really there in substance. As a result, your actions, both physical and mental, will move to bring about in reality the image you are visualizing.

During my university years at the U.S. Naval Academy at Annapolis—before I became a naval pilot—I underwent training in aircraft recognition. All of us sat at one end of a hall while silhouettes of American and foreign military aircraft were flashed on a screen at speeds similar to combat situations. We were supposed to write down the numerical designations and names of the planes, such as A-4 Skyhawk, F-11-F Tiger, MIG-21, and so forth. But the task became more difficult each week, because they kept adding more planes, scrambling the order, and speeding up the projection. Finally, it got ridiculous, because the images were going by faster than an MTV music video so that most of us saw only a blur, and some didn't see anything. I began to see planes that weren't even invented yet.

When it came time for the final exam, I didn't know for certain which planes I was seeing. I wrote down hunches, intuitions, and reflex responses. But when the test results were announced, virtually everyone had scored a perfect 100 percent. We had seen the planes, even if we didn't necessarily believe it. For me, that test proved that images can be stored and retained, unconsciously, at incredible speeds. And those stored images, when recalled, can enhance performance.

What about the thousands of flickering images we see on a TV, computer, or movie screen? What about commercials? Do we have to believe the products really do all those amazing things before we buy them? Do viewers have to think that violent scenes in movies and TV are actually occurring in real life for there to be a negative effect on their behavior? Many people believe that violent fantasy has no impact on their lives whatsoever, because they think they're too intelligent to be swayed by it. Well, I've got news for them. Whatever you see or experience, real or imagined, consciously or subliminally, when repeated vividly over and over, does affect your behavior, and definitely can influence you to buy a product or buy into a lifestyle, good or bad.

Your attitude and beliefs are, quite simply, functions of what you see day in and day out. Information can be taken in almost unnoticed. You won't react to it until later, and you still won't be aware of what lies behind your response. In other words, what you see really is what you get, regardless of whether you know it or not. You don't need to be watching images of airplanes, or TV shows, or music videos, video games, or commercials. You can be just lying down, or commuting to work, or walking through a park, and by seeing from within, in your mind's eye, you can change your life.

By rehashing fears and problems, you can make yourself depressed. As a result, you can botch a business deal, hurt a relationship, or lower your performance. By forecasting a gloomy outcome in your mind's eye, you can act as your own witch doctor and practice a modern-day kind of voodoo that will fulfill your negative prediction with uncanny accuracy. On the other hand, by replaying in your mind's eye the best game you ever played, you can repeat that best game again, when the stakes are even higher and the pressure is on. And by mentally pre-playing the best game you've ever imagined, you can set the stage for a world-class performance. This "instant replay" and "instant pre-play" applies to anything from a successful sales call or athletic event to the effective motivation of your team-mates and children.

Your attitudes and beliefs are the software programs driving you every day on life's journey. Breakthroughs in neuroscience have confirmed that neural pathways in your brain—physical highways loaded with electro-chemical messages, called "traffic"—can be rewired to create new images of achievement. New habits of excellence can be internalized, and virtual reality becomes reality. Thoughts do become things. Observation, imitation, repetition, internalization leads to realization. The Law of Attraction takes action, over time, to gain permanent traction!

"Know yourself" is one of the fundamental ideas of modern philosophy, with its origins in ancient civilizations. It stands to reason that before we can understand others and their motiva-tions, we need intimate insights into our own mental, physical, and emotional assets and liabilities. In order to gain the respect of others, we must first earn it. We must be respectable. In order to be a role model, we must first set a positive example. In order to lead others, we must first lead ourselves. In order to give oth-ers counsel, we must first counsel ourselves. We must look in the mirror when we ask who is responsible for our success or failure. We need to challenge our time-worn assumptions and prejudices and reflect on the vast potential within. If we lived a thousand years, we couldn't discover more than a fraction of our creative capabilities.

The acquisition of knowledge is a lifelong experience, not a collection of facts or skills. In decades past, what you learned in school was largely all you needed to learn. You could rely on that knowledge for the rest of your life. With knowledge expanding exponentially, this is no longer true. Hundreds of scientific papers are published daily. Every 30 seconds some new high-tech company produces yet another new innovation or application. Your formal education has a very short shelf life. A shared belief emerged from a recent round-table discussion among a group of some of the world's most successful business leaders. All these leaders, while innovating in their businesses, were doing the same in other spheres of their lives. They agreed that their organizations' ability to sustain a competitive advan-tage depended on the personal growth of their team leaders and team members, and that those who believed they had completed their educations were on a fast track to personal obsolescence. Lifelong learning, once a luxury, has become absolutely vital to continued success. Winners understand that yesterday's world records are today's entry-level requirements.

Question: Do you have to see it before you believe it, or believe before you can see it? (In other words, do you need hard evidence to support your beliefs, or do you put more emphasis on faith?)

Action: Think of something you believe to be true, based upon what others have told you. And think of something very important to you that you have seen with your own eyes, or experienced, that others may see differently. This will help you understand how each of us looks at life, through a filter based both on belief and experience. Discuss your responses with your colleagues.

PAST CONDITIONING EQUALS CURRENT PERFORMANCE

This book is about the desire for change and dissatisfaction with the status quo. I like where I am, but I see where I could go, and I want to be there. But how far and how high can I go? What are my limitations, psychologically? Limits are physical barriers. Limitations are psychological boundaries. I assert to you that you'll never reach your physical limits because of your psychological limitations.

Limits are physical, in that biological and other health factors, age, and skills do impose certain restrictions on performance. However, these limits—for most of us—will never be fully tested, because of the limitations caused by our beliefs. Limitations are psychological. Over time we all learn to raise or lower our expectations of ourselves because of our experiences. Disappointments become solid barriers. Successes give us confidence. As we get older, we don't simply move past these limitations we have internalized. Some of them stay with us throughout our lives. Winners are constantly seeking growth and high performance and, incrementally, keep raising the bar on these invisible barriers.

I recall when working with a world-class Olympic high jumper preparing for the Summer Games. He could clear the high-jump bar in practice and in competition at 7 feet, 3 inches. But no higher, regardless of the technique or practice. When he wasn't paying close attention one day, we raised the bar an inch to 7 feet, 4 inches. Thinking it was still at the lower setting, he cleared it. When I told him what he had done, he looked at me in disbelief, almost agitated. "But I can't jump that high," he exclaimed. "You just did," I smiled. "You just conquered your own four-minute mile barrier, just as Roger Bannister did so many years ago." Once Bannister proved that it was possible to run a mile in under four minutes, on May 6, 1954, suddenly more and more track stars were able to do it—proving an important lesson: once you stop believing something is impossible, it becomes possible.

When I was a boy I used to enjoy going to the local county fair to see the "flea circus" that was always a hit with me and my friends. I couldn't comprehend, at first, how those tiny fleas could be trained to hop and jump around on miniature trampolines, trapezes and not leap out of their little arenas that had no ceilings. I found out from the man that put on the show that, for a couple of weeks, he kept the fleas in a cardboard shoe box with a lid on it with pin-pricked holes so the fleas could breathe. Fleas normally can jump to a height of several feet; however, the "circus" fleas continually hit the box lid and soon learned that six inches was their maximum limit. When the lid was removed, because they had been trained to lower their expectations through frustration, they didn't even attempt to jump out of their circus arena, which would have been no problem.

We humans certainly are more intelligent than fleas, however behavior patterns seem to be consistent no matter the species. First we observe role models. We imitate their behavior. Through repetition, the imitation becomes habitual like brushing our teeth or driving our cars. If the feedback is negative and painful, we reinforce our failed attempts and settle for mediocrity rather than face future challenges and possible setbacks. If the feedback is positive and accepted as "target correction," we are motivated to try a different approach and keep reaching for our highest aspirations. Subconscious reflections of past mistakes, fears of future failures, and fears of the unknown tend to act as ceilings or lids on our achievements.

Here's the good news. While visiting Sea World many times with my grandchildren in my hometown of San Diego, California, my grandkids were amazed to see dolphins jumping in formation out of the water and over a rope positioned twelve feet above the surface. We learned from the trainers that they begin by placing a rope on the bottom of the pool and rewarding the dolphins with mackerel and tuna when they pass over it. Incrementally, the rope is raised until it is completely out of the water, and the dolphins are motivated by rewards to jump out of the water to cross over the rope. Just as dolphins are encouraged through positive reinforcement, people also respond to rewards, appreciation, recognition, and praise. Unlike animals, however, we humans have the power to choose and control, to a large degree, the conditioning of our present and future lives.

When you look in the mirror, there are three reflections: The child of your past, the person you are today, and the person you will become in the future. The way you were as a child, layered with the way you were 1, 5, 10, maybe 20 years ago equals your present behavior. You see, you condition yourself, and then you behave accordingly. The interesting thing—because past conditioning determines present performance—is that you never make a decision based upon what's happening right now. You base your decision on what happened before, the way it was, the way it used to be; and you're likely to experience the same thing again. So past conditioning equals present behavior. That's why Olympic athletes practice under a coach's watchful eyes, and then they perform based upon their training.

Well, how do you change? Interestingly enough, it isn't that present inputs determine future behavior. Oh, I wish it were. I wish you could go to a seminar and then just say, "I got it. I changed." You see, you get stimulated in the present, but your subconscious computer memory—if you're about 40 years old—is almost 350,000 hours full of past conditioning. So you go to a meeting for an hour. "Everybody got the new input? Have we all agreed to change?"

Could anyone presume that a pep talk would change some-body? Pep talks wear off. People go back to being themselves. That's why ongoing educational programs are so important. They become training and tracking systems for everyday living. Therefore, you look at your past conditioning, and you realize you've been limiting yourself. And you use present inputs to layer on top of the past conditioning, and you change the future behavior and performance accordingly; therefore, it's very important what you think about and practice over and over again. And it's most important that you view yourself as being self-limiting by your thinking and training, instead of blaming externals.

Most people feel like thermometers. A thermometer rises or falls to meet the external environment. It's controlled by outside circumstances. The majority of the population's self-images are controlled by society's external standards. Our self-image is the total picture of who we think we are; and the camera starts rolling at birth. The camera, our brain, takes pictures fast and furiously throughout life. And every frame is tucked away in a memory file of limitless capacity. This subjective sense of who we think ourselves to be governs all our actions and controls our destiny. How we feel about ourselves, how we rate our ability to hang in there to survive and win, and all that we ever do or aspire to be is based on our time-reinforced self-image. Unfortunately, once an idea or belief becomes a perception, it becomes a truth for our self-image. Each link we add to the growing chain of self-images may either strengthen or shackle our lives more tightly. Control is in our hands. We can't outgrow the limita-tions we place on ourselves through faulty self-imaging, but we can set new, higher standards. We can reset our self-image like an internal thermostat from low to high self-esteem, from loser to winner, and from victim of change to victor over change.

Each of us has a number of comfort zones or settings that we've developed throughout our lives that dictate the amount of discomfort we're willing to suffer before we make adjustments. Our self-image is very definitely a thermostat keeping us in a psychological comfort zone.

Over time we all learn to raise or lower our expectations of ourselves because of our experiences. Disappointments become solid barriers. Successes give us confidence. As we mature, we don't simply "outgrow" or move past these limitations we have internalized. Some of them stay with us throughout our lives.

Reflect for a moment on just how many of your behaviors are set into motion when you move out of these comfort zones. Too much can motivate as strongly as too little. On the level of conscious thought, there are any number of examples: How much time we feel comfortable in spending with those around us, how much effort we feel comfortable in expending on our daily tasks at the office or at home, how much money we feel comfortable in spending on our new clothes.

On a physical or physiological level, there are an infinite number of feedback systems that kick into gear when we leave this comfort zone. Much as a thermostat runs our home heating and cooling system, the body's hypothalamus, a tiny organ in the brain, senses body temperature. Venturing out on the hot side of the comfort zone, warm blood from inner core of the body is diverted by the hypothalamus in a wondrous manner that closes certain blood vessels and opens others near the surface of the skin where excess heat can be radiated away. Of course, the action of the hypothalamus in activating the sweat glands to return you to the comfort zone is no real surprise, but do you know why?

When perspiration evaporates from the surface of the skin, heat is removed; thus, sweating is a process that lowers body temperature. Moisten a portion of your hand and then blow on it. As the moisture evaporates, the skin is cooled. Is your hypothalamus getting the signal that you're dropping into the colder area of the comfort zone? No problem. Blood near the surface of the body is shunted inward to the core to conserve heat, and your muscles are set into rapid, small contractions to generate yet more heat. You call it shivering.

Perhaps the most amazing thermostat in our bodies has been uncovered in recent obesity research. We appear to have developed set points for body fat, a degree of body fatness that our bodies literally grow comfortable with. In as yet unknown ways, our bodies can sense and adjust both the rate at which we burn calories at rest, the basal metabolic rate, and the amount we eat. Early in our lives this stubborn fat thermostat is set by our levels of physical activity, our general eating habits, and genetic determinations. When we attempt to lose body fat solely through dietary means, eating fewer calories, our thermostat literally reduces the number of calories burned through basal metabolism. A drop of 500 calories a day in intake will be met by a corresponding drop in calories burned at rest, and the net result? You're eating less but burning less, and the body fat still taunts you.

Amazingly, when you gain small amounts of fat or simply turn up your caloric intake for several days, the body responds by turning up the thermostat; and the basal metabolic rate rises. You're eating more but burning more, and your weight remains fairly stable. Fortunately, for those of us wishing to change the setting of our thermostat, it can be done. Exercise is the key. Exercising enough to burn off an additional 200 calories a day can affect the resetting of the thermostat and start the fat loss process. When combined with healthy eating habits including dietary restriction as moderate as 200 calories a day, long-term fat loss can be achieved.

But why this lengthy discussion and digression into feedback and thermostat? Because our self-image is very definitely a thermostat keeping us in a psychological comfort zone. Our set point for winning is arrived at over time based on belief in ourselves, our abilities, and our worth. With a low self-image, however, our psychological thermostat is set correspondingly low. Not believing that he or she is capable of much or worth much, the low-image individual is comfortable with failure. When challenged to venture out on the high side or take a chance to change the status quo, he or she pulls back. "I'm not capable of that. That's beyond my meager abilities. It's not worth the effort. Why bother?" This is the way that negative self-talk goes.

With a strong and healthy belief in ourselves and what we're capable of, we can go out and survive the stress of day-to-day living and reaching worthy goals. When our comfort zone is set at high, we believe we can handle whatever is thrown at us. If we dare venture beyond our safety zone, we pull back. The risks are too great for who we think we are. If our efforts to win fall below the comfort zone, we feed back to our self-image some positive self-talk, "Next time I'll do it better. I can do that. Harder work and concentration will win me that prize."

At my seminars, I like to check a person's self-image when he or she first enters the meeting room. In this way I can determine the awareness and the needs of my audience. I remember a woman came into my seminar room and sat down in the first row. As she sat down, I said, "Good morning. Are you attending the seminar alone?" She answered, "No. I'm divorced." I said, "How long have you been single?" trying to sound nonjudgmental. She replied, "I've been divorced for two years now." And I asked another question, "Are the divorce proceedings still going on?" Well, she looked puzzled and said, "Why, no, of course not. I told you; it happened two years ago." I smiled reassuringly, "Well then, if you were divorced two years ago, you are single now."

What that woman learned during the seminar took me 35 years of self-doubt to figure out, and that is: You never carry a mistake or childhood labels or failure forward. You don't wear failure like a coat. The performer is always valuable, while the performances are learning experiences not to be repeated if negative and to be reinforced constantly if positive. Now, when new friends or associates ask our seminar graduate, "Are you married?" she answers unhesitatingly, "No, I'm not married." She's a powerful demonstration of the truth that we are what we see, what we do, and most important, what we think.

As we said earlier, when we look in the mirror, there are three reflections: The child of our past, the person we are today, and the person we will become. We can never totally erase experiences from our memories. If they were negative, our thermostats may be set at low performance or even no win. But we can reset our thermostats. With the right role models and the right self-talk, we can change the perceptions that have twisted and colored our image of who we really are.

WHAT IS YOUR TREASURE CHEST WITHIN?

Knowledge of your attributes, abilities, interests, strengths, weaknesses, and traits is essential to becoming proactive in career choice and career change. Where to begin your personal assessment? First you should know your innate talents. After many years of observation, we're still surprised by how few people try to make a connection between what they're good at and what they "do." Virtually all individuals have at least three to five major talents. Many have more. It is important to note that your talents are present at birth. You will gain knowledge, attitudes, skills, and habits throughout your life. Our careers are a blend of natural abilities, environmental modeling, acquired skills, and experience. Many times our careers hinge heavily on the economic requirements at pivotal age and family considerations. If we are to develop our lives along the path of greatest wisdom, however, we should give serious thought to discovering our inherent abilities as early as possible.

One of the secrets to becoming a consistent winner in your personal and professional life is to play to your core competencies. To be your best, you need to do what you love, love what your do, and deliver more in value than you expect to receive in payment. You must believe in your potential, and that's what this program is designed to help you discover and employ. How do you know what it is? In addition to your own introspection, you should consider investing in a legitimate talent or natural gifts test. Two non-profit foundations are worth considering: The Johnson O'Connor Foundation in New York City, with multiple offices nationwide, and The Ball Foundation in the Chicago area, with an online program as well. There are 19 innate talents that have been identified and can be tested. Google their names for more information. You have literally acres of diamonds inherently waiting for you to uncover and mine them. When you look for value, look inside!

The next step in assessing your interests is considering your current ones. What do you most enjoy after work? What do you most want to do on weekends and vacations? What are your hobbies? Your after-work activities? Your favorite kinds of books? Examination of your personal interests might reveal a gem of potential you can apply to your current professional work. Also, our research has shown that what we love and do well as children continues to shape our lives as adults. So an excellent awareness exercise is to spend time reviewing positive experiences and fantasies you had as a child.

Talents and personality traits come naturally at birth. Behavior patterns and habits are learned by observation, imitation, and repetition. In all of the best research involving high-performance executives in nearly every field and job description—from technical to sales, from top management to hourly workers—combined with a database working with Olympic athletes, coaches, and professional teams, we have learned that certain core behavioral traits generally define the high achiever and leader. For example, you want high scores in ambition, self-confidence, and mental toughness. Candidates who score low on any of these three traits or whose tests show a lack of self-control of habits, lack of flexibility, and a pattern of becoming overly emotional under stress may require careful screening or special training to predict their probable impact on performance.

Even if you're reasonably satisfied with the current status of your career and your life, exploring yourself as deeply as possible can increase your self-awareness and your motivation. And if you do know what you really want to do—and it involves changes—ask whether you are acting to make your dreams a reality. Champions know who and where they are today, and what and where they want to be tomorrow. And they get there.

Question: What do honestly think is holding you back the most in achieving your highest aspirations? Externals beyond your control, or internal insecurities?

Action: Get out of your comfort zone. Call, text, email, or reach out to someone in person who you are hesitant to contact because of time, distance, or misunderstanding.

THE ONE AND ONLY YOU

Authentic champions are those individuals who in a very natural, free-flowing way seem to consistently get what they want from life by providing valuable service to others. They put themselves together across the board—in their personal, professional, and community lives. They set and achieve goals that benefit others as well as themselves. You don't have to get lucky to win at life, nor do you have to knock other people down or gain at the expense of others.

Winning is taking the talent or potential you were born with, and have since developed, and using it fully toward a purpose that makes you feel worthwhile according to your own internal standards. Happiness, then, is the natural by-product of living a worthwhile life. Happiness is the natural experience of winning your own self-respect, as well as the respect of others. You can't buy it, wear it, drive it, swallow it, inject it, or travel to it! Happiness is the journey, not the destination. Winners are those whose "inner hard drive" carries a message something like this: "I can do a variety of things pretty well. I can try new challenges and be successful. When things don't go smoothly at first, I keep trying or get more information to do it in a different way until it works out right." These are the few, like yourself, who can and usually do learn the most and who can give the most to others from what they've learned. They've discovered that their imaginations serve as a life-governing device—that, if your self-image can't possibly see yourself doing something or achieving something, you literally cannot do it! It's not what you are that holds you back, it's what you think you're not.

To develop to your fullest potential, begin by consciously avoiding the temptation to judge yourself against the fantasies presented by the media, especially those of television commercials and motion pictures. Reality says you have the potential to become infinitely more than you are now. Animals are programmed by instinct, but we human beings can develop abilities through observation, imitation, and reasoning. As we have discussed, the greatest limitations you will ever face will be those you place on yourself. The power of others to rain on your parade and stifle your self-image is awesome for most people. The good news is that you don't have to take on the role of victim. You can rewrite your scenario and become a victor in the drama called life. You are your own scriptwriter, and the play is never finished, no matter what your age, position, or station in life.

This "behind the mirror" introspection begins by realizing that skin color, birthplace, religious beliefs, gender, financial status, and intelligence are not measures of worth or worthiness. It is accepting the fact that every human being is a distinctly unique individual—and thinking how good that is! We are unique in our fingerprints. Unique in our footprints, lip-prints, and in our eye-prints. Each of us also speaks with a sound frequency unmatched by any other person.

You spend your life learning, exploring, growing, losing, winning, and, if you are unselfish, trying to make a positive contribution. Your life is a collection of moments and memories. It also is the legacy you pass on to family and future leaders. The lessons you leave in your own, next generation—as core values—are far more priceless than the material valuables you will leave them in your estate. Life is governed by universal laws that have remained unchanged since the beginning of recorded time. Actions cause reactions. Rights carry responsibilities. Truth promotes trust. Thoughts become things. Love is to life as the sun is to planet Earth. Every choice carries a reward or consequence. In the long run, like rings within a tree, each of us becomes the sum total of our actions.

The greatest men and women in all walks of life achieved their greatness out of a desire to express something within themselves that had to be expressed. Successful people— successful in the deepest sense of the word—don't look for achievements that will bring them the most for the least amount of effort. They look for the greatest challenges to test their potential. In considering your own potential, realize that success and fulfillment choices in your life far exceed what you may currently think is possible. And our concept of "possible" is always expanding! Just recently, scientists at the Salk Institute for Biological Studies in La Jolla, California, discovered that the memory storage capacity of our brains is ten times what they had previously thought—now, a petabyte, which is equivalent to 500 billion pages of text! This begs the question, what are you storing in your mental library? Don't limit your thinking! Do not impose mental obstacles before you give yourself (and your brain) an opportunity to explore possibilities and believe in the champion in *you!*

I was in Dubai for a business meeting recently and was introduced to the flying drone taxi service from the airport. You pay by smartphone or credit card, dial in the address you are going to in the GPS onboard computer, you fasten your seat belt, and the pilotless drone takes you up and over the rush hour traffic to your destination in a few minutes, instead of the normal bumper to bumper one-hour ride. While I realized drones had many applications, I assumed that—like driverless cars—it would take several years to make flying taxi drones commercially viable. What appeared to be science fiction only a year or two ago has now become science fact!

The invisible barriers contained in your attitude and beliefs are, quite simply, functions of what you see day in and day out. Information can be taken in almost unnoticed. You won't react to it until later, and you still may not be aware of what lies behind your response. You don't need to be watching a computer screen or TV. You can be lying down with your eyes closed, or commuting to work, or walking through a park or at the beach or lake. By seeing from within your role in being a change master, instead of a change victim, you can literally change your life. That's the power you have at your command.

We all yearn to shape our own lives, fashion our own destinies. But most of us find ourselves in the same dilemma from our teens onward. How do we really want to spend our days? What choices should we make? What habit changes do we need to make? What can we do that will fill our lives with meaning and bring us the adventure and rewards we are seeking? How do we know we've chosen the right career and the proper goals? Who should our role models be today?

This journey begins with pinpointing where you stand today on your career path, not where you wish or hoped you'd be. To know other people takes intelligence. To know yourself takes wisdom. By exploring yourself as deeply as possible, you will expand your opportunities for leading a life of significance and fulfillment. When you know where you are today, you will be able to employ the winning techniques in this course to create a new tomorrow.

Here are some action steps to help you gain more self-awareness, so that you can reach your goal of breaking your invisible barriers and setting yourself free:

Get a journal, if you don't already have one.

Use it to define your character, as if you had been given an assignment to publish an autobiography of the person you'd most like to become.

Begin by asking yourself and writing your responses to:

"If there were no constraints of money, time, or circumstance, what would I begin doing tomorrow?"

In order to answer that important question, use these other key questions as guides:

What did you love to do as a child?

Are you enjoying your personal and professional life and expressing your talents in a way that is fulfilling?

Write down everything you can think of that is good about yourself.

Make sure you've identified your talents and abilities, and your unique personality and character traits.

Write down the important role models, mentors, contacts, springboards, and sounding boards in your sphere of influence.

Put all this in your journal—really make your life and your dreams an open book—and then turn the journal entries into phone calls, texts, e-mails, proposals, applications—and actions!

Schedule a comprehensive physical exam from a reputable clinic at least once a year.

Maintenance of your only transportation life vehicle, your body, is vital.

Don't wait for the problem to surface.

Engage in prevention.

Also, study the health history of your close relatives. Their predispositions and longevity pros and cons can offer you valuable insights into your own outlook and vulnerability.

Break the daily and weekly routine you have set.

Stretch your comfort zone and get out of that comfortable rut.

Unplug the TV for a month.

Meet some new friends.

Join a positive online community.

Check your knowledge sources as to their validity.

Engage in some different weekend and after-work activities.

Make a list of "I Am's," two columns: assets or "I Am Good At," in one column; liabilities or "I Need Improvement" in the other column.

Pick your ten best traits and your ten traits needing most improvement.

Take the first three liabilities and schedule an activity or find a winner who will help you improve in each of the three areas.

Forget about the rest of the liabilities.

Relish and dwell on all ten of your best assets. They'll take you anywhere you want to go in life.

Look at yourself through other people's eyes.

Imagine being your spouse or partner.

Imagine being your parents.

Imagine being your child or children.

Imagine being your boss or employee. How do you think each of those individuals would describe you?

Step back from the canvas of your own life and consider the kind of people who are attracted to you and the kind of people to whom you are attracted.

Are they the same type?

Do you attract winners?

Are you attracted to people who are more or less successful than yourself? Why?

Listen for truth and speak the truth. Don't let the ads and the fads make you one of the countless victims of greed or tunnel vision. When you read something that impresses you, check the source. When in doubt, call the research department of a national publication you trust or call a major university you respect. If it really works wonders, it will be available everywhere, like aspirin. If it's a breakthrough, look for it to be announced by reputable news authorities and government agencies. Rather than hearing what you want to hear, listen for the facts of the matter. Remember, everything you think is your opinion, based upon your impressions from limited sources. Keep expanding your sources from the best authorities. View everything with a certain open-minded skepticism, to explore it without prejudice, yet skeptical enough to research and test its validity.

Take thirty precious minutes each day for you alone. Use this extra half hour of your life to wake up and live. Use this time to answer the question: How can I best spend my time today on priorities that are important to me? Be completely aware and honest that your life belongs to you and that all that exists in your life is seen out of your own eyes and experienced by your own mind and body. Turn every mental crisis you are now facing into an opportunity for more personal growth.

Question: Think about it over the weekend. If there were no constraints of money, time, or circumstance, what would you begin doing tomorrow?

Action: Enroll in, investigate, research, and begin to pursue something that has been a lifelong dream of yours. It could be a hobby, a home-based business, community service, or a new career path.

The greatest limitations you
will ever face will be those
you place on yourself.

––––––––––––––––––––––––––––

You always project on the outside
how you feel on the inside.

Chapter 2

The Inner Winner:
Intrinsic Core Values

THE MOST IMPORTANT
HUMAN QUALITY

ealthy self-esteem is perhaps the most important and basic quality of a winning human being. You want to be able to say, "I like myself. Given my parents and my background, I'm glad I'm me. I realize I may not be the best-looking in the group, but I always look my best in every group. I'd rather be me than anyone else in the world." This is the self-talk of a winner. Winners have developed a strong sense of self-worth, regardless of their status. They weren't necessarily born with these good feelings, but they've learned to like themselves through practice.

The most successful companies in the world know that valued employees are their most precious resource. Valuable employees pass their value on to customers. The result? Excellence. Quality. The most powerful competitors in the world marketplace. Instead of comparing ourselves to others, we should view ourselves in terms of our own abilities, interests, and goals. We can begin by making a conscious effort to upgrade our lifestyle, education, and personal development. You always project on the outside how you feel on the inside.

Self-acceptance, as we are right now, is the key to healthy self-esteem—seeing ourselves as worthwhile, changing, imperfect, growing individuals, and knowing that although we aren't born with equal mental and physical uniforms, we are born with the equal right to feel deserving of excellence according to our own internal standards. A healthy challenge is to accept ourselves right now as changing, growing, imperfect works of art and also form an image or dream of who we are becoming. This future projection is in no way designed to detract from the magnificence and beauty of who we are now. It gives us direction and inspiration to become more of who we really are.

Core values radiate like rings, as when a leaf falls in a pond. The self-centered constantly seek approval from and power over others. They try to impress them with their worth rather than express concern for others' well-being. And their outward appearances usually involve ways to hide their real thoughts and intentions. There is a paradoxical proverb here: You must feel worthy of the best, but not more worthy than the rest. In other words, you were born with every right to experience success, but being your best doesn't mean that you are superior to others.

The value-centered give of themselves freely and graciously, constantly seeking to empower others. Open and modest, they have no need for conceit, the opposite of core value. Feeling good about who they are, and not needing to constantly talk about their victories or line their walls with associations with celebrities or their awards, people with core values spend much of their time "paying value" to others, a concept you'll learn more about throughout this book.

When praised, they accept the value paid and share the spotlight. When they make mistakes, they view them as learning experiences and accept responsibility.

Self-esteem can't be bought, won in an arena, measured by a stock portfolio, or displayed in a fashion model's figure or an entertainment star's profile. Self-esteem is a profound belief that you deserve to be happy and successful. It is as necessary for human development as oxygen, as basic as the carbon from which diamonds are formed. I used to think that diamonds were so sought after because of their glittering appearance as a status symbol, but I discovered that they're actually so valuable because they're almost impossible to destroy. Formed at the earth's core and very rare, they hold their value indefinitely.

The simple truth is that if you have no internalized feelings of value, you have nothing to share with others. You can need them, depend on them, look for security in them—but you can't share or give feelings of love and value to anyone else unless you possess these feelings yourself. The diamond is inside, as an uncut gemstone of priceless potential, waiting to be mined, shaped, and polished. You are the star in your own universe, and, with the help of this book, you are about to discover the essence of your unique journey toward personal enrichment.

DISCOVERING THE AUTHENTIC CHAMPION WITHIN

You're standing on the highest pedestal, the one in the center. You hear the roar of approval from the crowd. As the first note of the national anthem is played in the Olympic stadium, you feel all the pride and honor that accompanies this moment. Ten thousand hours of preparation for this one triumphant moment in history. You've won the gold!

That dream of an Olympic championship is in the heart of every amateur athlete, just as the Grand Final, World Cup, Super Bowl, and Wimbledon are the goals of professional football players and tennis players. What are your dreams? You're most likely not a world-class athlete, but surely you have aspirations of your own. Perhaps you imagine a metaphorical gold medal being placed around your neck by the Managing Director or CEO of your company, or by your friends and family for being the best in your own unique way. Maybe you wonder whether you're up to the risk of starting your own business.

There is a trap of having to prove your worth. Let me explain. On Sundays, my grandparents would take us children to ride the huge merry-go-round next to the zoo. We could hardly wait to mount those bobbing zebras, lions, tigers, and stallions, and whirl round and round to the music of the antique pipe organ. Surrounded by mirrors and lights, our hearts would pound in anticipation as we stretched out desperately, trying to be the one among all the riders who would grab the gold ring and win another ride. So began our competitive spirits. You may never even have heard of grabbing the gold ring on the carousel, but in many cities where there are carousels, if you reach out and catch it, you not only get a free ride—your name is also announced over the loudspeaker and all the other kids and their parents applaud. And, of course, the kids all wish it could have been them instead of you.

Reflecting back now on my youth, I've come to some realizations. Many of us did start out thinking of success and winning as something that you got by reaching outside yourself and proving to others that you were worthy. Come to think of it, most of my friends also believed that you had to prove, earn, win, or perform in some special way, and then you would deserve the gold ring or the Olympic gold medal. The approval of others seemed to precede feelings of self-confidence and self-worth. You were entitled to feel good about yourself only after you performed well. Why did it take me so many years to discover that just the reverse ought to be true?

After devoting most of my career to investigating the well-springs of personal and professional success, I'm able to make the following statements with great confidence: You need to feel love inside yourself before you can offer it to anyone else. Your own sense of value determines the quality of your performance. Performance is only a reflection of internal worth, not a measure of it. The less you try to impress, the more impressive you are. What you show the world on the outside is a mirror image of how you feel on the inside.

The key trait shared by athletic champions and winners in every walk of life is the fundamental belief in one's own internal value. If your success depends on external possessions, you'll be subject to constant anxiety. When your peer group cheers one of your accomplishments, you'll feel good for a while, but then you'll wonder if they'll cheer as loudly the next time. If they're critical, you will feel hurt and threatened. The truth is, you can never win over a long period of time if your concept of success depends upon the perfect performance or the placing of a gold medal around your neck.

It's obvious that talent, looks, and other attributes aren't equally distributed, but we're all given an abundance of value—more than we could use in several lifetimes. The game of life certainly isn't played on a level playing field for each of us in terms of education, a supportive home life, and other circumstances beyond our control, but we can assure you that you were born with the qualities of a champion. That's what we mean by value.

You see, champions are born, but they can be unmade by their perceptions, exposure, and responses. Losers are not born to lose. They're programmed that way by their own responses to their environment and their decisions. There's a phrase we like to use—the Inner Winner—that describes the kind of person who recognizes his or her internal value and is able to use that recognition as the foundation for achieving any goal. The secret of wearing the gold medal around your neck in the external world is that first you must be an Inner Winner. You must recognize that you're already a champion within.

Question: Do you feel good about who you are today, or do you feel you need to excel more to prove your worth?

Action: Give yourself a reward for something you have done, that you are proud of, even though no one around you may have noticed or commented.

THE FOUR LEGS OF VALUE

An ancient Chinese proverb tells us, "A child's life is like a piece of paper on which every passerby leaves a mark." We cannot teach our children self-esteem. We can only help them discover it within themselves by adding positive marks and strokes on their slates. My own belief is that we're all born with as much potential as we'll ever have, but our early years can squeeze out feelings of self-worth and self-esteem like an electric juicer. Most psychologists say it starts in infancy, when parents are or are not able to respond appropriately to a baby's needs and reflect back to the baby that they see, respond to, and accept the baby as he or she really is. Tiny infants can be made to feel that their demands are excessive, burdensome, not worthy of full attention, and can respond by asking for and, worse, expecting less. Comparison is only part of the equation, and this begins as soon as they're old enough to hear parents, peers, and teachers compare them with others. Once started, the erosion of self-esteem often picks up speed in high school. In training videos I produce within various high schools and colleges, some students slump in their chairs, staring at their hands. Others reveal how little they think of themselves (as well as their fellow students) by interrupting with "cute" remarks or boisterous chatter. The attempts to hide a fragile self-image are most obvious among those who affect the cool look or who display disdain. And, of course, bullying by cruel students both in school and via the Internet can have devastating, long-term effects on students who don't fit into the "cool" category.

I remember my own youth, how eager we were to belong to the "in" group. Sometimes I went to extremes, clowning around in efforts to impress the most popular girls and boys. I felt wonderful when I was accepted, distraught when I was ignored or rejected. With the greater emphasis today on material and physical appearances, young people seem even more driven to vie for their peers' attention and recognition, as if buying or crashing their way into the winner's circle were the key to the good life. However, there's a critical difference between having to prove yourself—wanting to be the best to make up for inadequate self-esteem—and seeking to manifest inner worth and value, being your best for the pure exhilaration of excellence. We all struggle with these two forms of expression, myself included. One reason I've spent much of my adult life studying human behavior is that I want answers to the questions for myself, especially the difference between winners and losers—about which I had cause to wonder early in my own youth.

All positive motivation is rooted in self-esteem—the development of which, just as with other skills, takes practice. And that practice, as with other forms of it, must be carefully structured. Think of self-esteem as a four-legged chair. Imagine you're sitting on it right now and looking in the mirror. Do you respect the person you see? Is it someone you really want to be? Are you doing what you want to personally and professionally?

Are you going where you want to go? Are you in charge of your life? An unhesitating "yes" to a majority of these questions suggests your self-esteem is in good shape. Negative answers indicate you should watch and listen with particular attention.

First, We All Need a Sense of Belonging

Returning to the image of the chair, the first leg of self-esteem is a sense of belonging. We all have a deep-rooted need to feel we're a part of something larger than ourselves. This need, which psychologists call an affiliation drive, encompasses people, places, and possessions. Our instinct for belonging—for being wanted, accepted, enjoyed, and loved by close ones—is extremely powerful. It explains the bond of an extended family, friends, and teammates. It also explains why some adolescents join gangs. They want to belong, even if it's wrong.

Children should be proud of their family heritage in a home where they feel safe, loved, and welcome. Home also should be a place where children want to bring their friends, rather than a place they want to leave as soon as possible. This applies to your adult professional life as well, in whatever organizational structure you find yourself.

Second, a Sense of Individual Identity

The second leg, which complements the sense of belonging, is a sense of individual identity. No human being is exactly like another, not even an identical twin. We are all unique combinations of talents and traits that never existed before and will never exist again in quite the same package. Leaders stand out particularly for knowing who they are, having confidence in what they believe, and feeling respect for their present lives as well as for their potential. Children should be observed as they grow and play—their learning styles, what they love to do in their free time, and discovery of their unique positive talents so these can be nurtured into skills. Report cards don't necessarily measure talents. They often are a measure only of discipline, memory, and attention span. Companies also are moving away from check-off list performance reviews for a particular job description, to observe what team members are contributing to the success of the organization.

Third, a Sense of Worthiness

The third leg of self-esteem is a sense of worthiness, the feeling that I'm glad I'm me, with my genes and background, my body, my unique thoughts. Even if others make you feel you belong, even if others praise you, you won't feel very worthy if you violate your own values. (This isn't limited to individuals. One of the basic missions of top multi-national corporations is nourishing a sense of worth through improved quality and excellence.)

Without our own approval, we have little to offer. If we don't feel worth loving, it's hard to believe that others love us; instead, we tend to see those others as appraisers or judges of our value.

People who feel undeserving of love because their self-esteem is marginal, easily hurt those who do love them. Insecurity generates the jealousy, excessive possessiveness, and compulsion to turn trifles into tragedies that often ruin caring relationships.

If you were lucky enough to have parents who taught you the importance of responsibility, honesty, initiative, courage, faith, self-control, and most of all, love, please remember to say a frequent prayer of thanks. Many of us were less fortunate—but we can still build our own values by asking ourselves the right questions. Are the trappings of your lifestyle more important to you than your inner values? Is making a good impression more important than being true to yourself? Do you constantly feel you must prove your worth with outer achievements? Do you feel guilty when you're praised or when you indulge yourself in some selfish pleasure?

A sense of belonging, identity, and worthiness can only be rooted in intrinsic core values as opposed to outer, often material, motivation. Without them, we depend on others constantly to fill our leaking reserves of self-esteem—but also tend to suspect others of ulterior motives. Unable to accept or reject others' opinions for what they're worth, we are defensive about criticism and paranoid about praise—and no amount of praise can replace the missing qualities. A healthy sense of belonging, identity, and worthiness is also essential to belief in your dreams. It is most essential during difficult times, when you have only a dream to hang on to.

The Fourth Leg: A Sense of
Control and Competence

Early in my career in motivational psychology, I thought the chair of self-esteem balanced firmly on those three legs, especially since they involved intrinsic core values. It took much time and research to realize that a fourth leg—one of the most important—was missing.

There are many reasons why few individuals currently in high school and college believe they were born to win. The supportive extended family—in many cases, even the nuclear family—is disappearing. Role models are increasingly unhealthy. The commercial media bombards young senses ever more insistently with crime, hedonism, and other unhealthy forms of escape. But whatever the explanation, constructive leaders cannot emerge and develop without the creative imagination that serves them like fuel—which is why the apprehension, frustration, and hesitation I see and hear among a significant number of our younger generation is cause for concern. At the moment, the future they imagine will help drive neither happiness nor success.

The chair's fourth leg is self-efficacy, a functional belief in your ability to control what happens to you in a changing, uncertain world. A sense of worthiness may give you the emotional means to venture, but you need self-efficacy, the sense of competence and control, to believe you can succeed. And that belief can't develop without confidence that you can make a difference.

Self-efficacy is essentially confidence in your personal power—not the power to control or dominate others, but power in the richly creative sense of self-empowerment: of being able to do successfully what you set out to do. With a sense of self-efficacy in place, mind and body join in the journey toward the goal as an inventor, artist, executive, teacher, nurturing parent, or young student.

In theory, once a goal is attained, it no longer serves the same purpose. An entrepreneur who has found investors willing to advance sufficient capital to launch a new business doesn't keep looking for venture capital. However, self-efficacy is an exception. Empowering you to strive for your goals, it also continues motivating you after you've reached the initial objectives.

That's why it is so important to assign responsibility for outcomes to the people involved. The more success they experience, the stronger their confidence grows—and the more responsibility they want to assume. In an increasingly competitive global marketplace, each member of the workforce simply must believe that he or she is a team leader, a "quality individual" who expresses that quality in excellent production and service. With increasing pressures on profit and the need to do more with fewer workers, it's essential to raise the value of the employees' stock in themselves.

That's also why it is very important to assign small tasks to your children as early as possible so they can learn that their choices and efforts result in consequences and successes. The more success they experience, the stronger their confidence grows—and the more responsibility they want to assume. Children growing up, regardless of their parents' income, should be given specific household chores and duties they can accomplish and be proud of. Each of us needs to learn that problems and setbacks are just temporary inconveniences and learning experiences. The idea that setbacks are not failures, but course corrections, needs to be constantly reinforced.

Armed with a view of failure as a learning experience, children can develop an early eagerness for new challenges and will be less afraid to try new skills. Although they appreciate compliments, they benefit most from their own belief that they are making a valuable contribution to life, according to their own internal standards.

Children learn what they live and live what they learn. And so do we, their adult role models.

Question: Do you have a tendency to complete projects, solve problems, and take actions that others should do but bring to you instead?

Action: When someone in your family or organization asks you to solve a problem for them, first ask them what they think should be done, and then help coach them to follow through.

The following are examples of what we refer to as characteristics of low self-esteem and high self-esteem. As you read them, check your own responses as they apply to you:

EXAMPLES OF LOW SELF-ESTEEM

Criticizing Others: Pointing out weaknesses in others so it can make them feel better about themselves.

Criticizing Self: Thinking and talking about themselves in a negative way. Using put-downs and focusing on what they can't do or are unable to do. Only focusing on the "negative" aspects of self.

Attack and Prove: Attacking another person and gathering information to support that attack. The information can come from "evidence" they find or from other people's opinions.

Live by Comparison: Constantly comparing themselves to other people and evaluating whether they are doing well or not according to how others are performing.

Arrogant and Materialistic: Using material possessions, what they have, as evidence of their self-worth and success. Relying on external factors to prove their worth.

Quick Fixes and Fads: Looking for the quickest way out of a situation or following a fashion whereby they don't think for themselves.

Poor Personal Hygiene: Grooming and how they present is not important. Their outward presentation is a reflection of inward perception.

CHARACTERISTICS OF HIGH SELF-ESTEEM

Worth Based on Internal Values: They have an understanding as to what is important for them in their inner world and their feelings of self-esteem are founded on that.

View Failures as Learning Experiences: When these people have a "failure," they appreciate that there is another opportunity to succeed around the corner and this time they can learn something, so it doesn't occur again.

Take Differences of Opinion (without feeling rejected): As those with higher self-esteem are stronger in their self-opinion, they're not as affected by other people's opinions or judgments that may be directed toward them.

Laugh at Their Situation (without self-ridicule): The ability to laugh at yourself, your misgivings, your shortcomings, and your mistakes is a sign of high self-esteem. These people don't trivialize themselves; they just appreciate that there is no point dramatizing themselves.

Express Opinions, Even If Controversial: Ability to have a level of certainty within themselves so when they put forward their own opinion, they are confident with their perspective. This manifests in meetings and in the way that people respond in teams where they have the confidence to say what they are thinking.

Enjoy Being Alone, Without Loneliness: Being comfortable with your own company is a symptom of high self-esteem. You don't have to even be doing anything, just sitting can be enough.

Appreciate Others' Opinions and Achievements (without jealousy): When a person can rejoice in other people's success, it is a reflection of their high self-esteem and how they feel comfortable within themselves.

Express, Without Trying to Impress: Ability to put forward ideas without needing approval or recognition for their opinion or for what they are saying.

SELF-ESTEEM UNLOCKS
YOUR POTENTIAL

Healthy self-esteem is a deep-down, inside-the-soul belief in your own worth, regardless of your age, looks, ethnicity, gender, religion, background, or status. It encompasses the idea that you have potential for success and fulfillment, and that you are worth investing in, learning, gaining skills, and performing a valuable service to society in your own, unique way.

It allows you to feel deserving of a new, healthier environment or lifestyle, instead of being a mirror or victim of your early or current circumstances. It is one of the most important roots in the healthy growth of every human being. Self-esteem gives you permission to believe you can improve and better yourself and becomes your passport, allowing you the freedom to journey as far as you dare, to seek a destiny worthy of your highest aspirations. It embraces where you want to go, rather than where you are coming from.

The late Dr. Nathaniel Branden, a friend and colleague of mine and a leading authority on healthy self-esteem, taught that to grow in self-esteem is to grow in the conviction we are competent to live and are worthy of happiness. And to face life with confidence, benevolence, and optimism. In this way, we're best able to reach our goals and experience fulfillment. To grow in self-esteem is to expand our capacity for happiness. If you understand this, you can see why all of us have a stake in cultivating our self-esteem, not merely those whose self-esteem is painfully low. We don't have to hate ourselves to learn to love ourselves more. We don't have to feel inferior to want to feel more competent. We don't have to be miserable to want to expand our capacity for joy.

The higher your self-esteem, the better equipped you are to cope with life's adversities. The higher your self-esteem, the more likely it is that you'll be innovative rather than ritualistic and tradition-bound in your work. And this ensures greater success in a world of increasingly rapid change. The higher your self-esteem, the more ambitious you tend to be. Not necessarily in a career or a financial sense, but more broadly, in creative and spiritual terms. With high self-esteem, you're more likely to form nourishing rather than destructive relationships. Like is drawn to like. Health is attracted to health. And vitality and expansiveness are more appealing than emptiness and frustration. With high self-esteem, you're more inclined to treat others with respect and goodwill, since you don't perceive them as threats and since self-respect is the foundation of respect for others. With high self-esteem, you experience more joy in the sheer fact of being, in waking up in the morning, and in living inside your own skin. These are just a few of the rewards of self-confidence and self-respect.

Self-esteem on whatever level is an intimately personal experience. It resides in the core of our being. It is what I think and feel about myself. Not what someone else thinks or feels. No one else can breathe for us. No one else can think for us. No one else can give us self-esteem. I can be loved by my family, my mate, my friends, and yet not love myself. I can be admired by my associates and yet regard myself as worthless. I can project assurance and poise that fools virtually everyone while I secretly tremble with a sense of my inadequacy. I can fulfill the expectations of others and yet fail my own. I can win every honor and yet feel I've accomplished nothing. I can be adored by millions and yet wake up each morning with a sickening sense of fraudulence and emptiness.

These ideas of Dr. Nathaniel Branden, which I have paraphrased, are powerful and proven. To win success without attaining positive self-esteem is to feel like an impostor, anxiously awaiting exposure. You see, the acclaim of others doesn't create our self-esteem. Neither does knowledge, skill, expertise, material possessions, a marriage, parenthood, charitable endeavors, sexual conquests, or a facelift. They can sometimes make us feel better about ourselves temporarily, or more comfortable in particular situations, but comfort is not self-esteem. The tragedy of many people's lives is that they look for self-confidence and self-respect in every direction except within and so they fail in their search. When you begin to understand self-esteem in this way, you can appreciate how foolish it is to think that only by making a more positive impression on others, you can enjoy a good self-regard.

You'll stop telling yourself, "If only I get one more promotion, if only I become a better wife and mother, if only I'm perceived to be a good provider, if only I can afford a bigger car, if only I could write a book, acquire another company, one more lover, one more award, one more acknowledgment of my selflessness, then I'll be ready to really feel at peace with myself." You see, this is an irrational quest and if you take it, your longing will always be for one more.

When you reach the pinnacle of self-esteem, you have an inner standard for judging your performance. You're sure of what you can do, and the opinion of others does not hold you an emotional hostage. Above all, you have a very precious commodity called self-respect. If you wanted to state your personal code of self-respect it might sound like this: I am valuable because I was created with an inner value and worth. I do not have to earn it. I nurture self-respect as I understand and internalize my basic inner value. The value is there. I don't have to achieve it. I already have it. My challenge is to nurture and protect it from getting jaded or twisted by the values of a "success at any cost" oriented society. If I can avoid the trap of trying to possess success or adorn myself with success at the expense of others, I can easily live with self-respect. It will be more important to me to do things to project my value, the marvelous gift I've been given, to other people. That is the primary motivation for being the best I can be. My worth is my word. I make commitments, and I do what I say I will do; this is more than just important to me, it is crucial.

I say to others, "I am valuable as you are valuable. We will make a value exchange. I will offer you the best I have, and I assume you will give me your best in return." People who see little or no value in themselves will not operate according to such a code. In fact a code like this may be distasteful to them. Instead of being concerned with self-respect, they'll try to gain recognition from others through manipulation, half-truth, and show.

The principle of feeling worthy and making others feel worthy also is a basic lesson to be practiced between loved ones. It is also one of the basic goals that I see across the globe as corporations everywhere pursue their search for excellence. The inner applause you give yourself when you succeed outweighs anything anyone could ever give you. People who live with a good sense of worthiness in themselves and others are people who understand and believe in personal values.

Parents and children in today's global society have a confused concept of self-esteem. The messages from all forms of media suggest that self-esteem is having a big ego and being able to assert ourselves as important in a celebrity-oriented, materialistic culture. Many people wrongly assume that self-esteem is the way we look, how much money we have, and how popular we are. In other words, the essence of self-esteem is lost and mixed up with self-indulgence and self-absorption. Instead of non-material, inner value, the concept of self-esteem has become narcissistic, hedonistic, and more associated with external "lifestyle" rather than feeling worthy of happiness and fulfillment.

We have the ability to edit and reprogram our bad memories—so they don't hold us back. We also have the ability to edit, reprogram, splice in, and spruce up our good memories—so they propel and launch us forward. We can begin by making a conscious effort to upgrade our attitudes, education, habits, and personal-development skills. We always project on the outside how we feel on the inside. We, ourselves, are our most influential coaches and critics of our performance. By rewiring our brains with positive, success-related messages, we can change our future outcomes. Let's review the fundamentals of healthy self-esteem:

Healthy self-esteem, or the lack of it, is at the root of most behavior, both positive and negative. Self-esteem is a combination of self-worth and self-trust. Self-worth is being glad you're you, with your genes, your body, your background, and your potential. Self-trust is the functional belief in your own ability positively and effectively to control what happens to you in a world of uncertainty. The first gives you a feeling of optimism. The second gives you empowerment.

No opinion and no judgment is so vitally important to your own growth and development as that which you hold of yourself. The most important conversations, briefings, meetings, and lectures you will ever have are those that you mull over in the privacy of your own mind. When you talk to yourself, speak as if you were encouraging your best friend. Talk to yourself with all due respect!

No eyes will ever critique a video of you, a selfie or photo of you, a reflection of you in a store window, or a full-length view of you in the mirror as you step out of the shower, as sharply and critically as your own eyes. Make an effort to feel good about your physical self, including what you eat, how you exercise, your grooming, how you dress, and how you think. If you don't feel good about any of those things, take control and join a support group with similar goals to make positive changes. Engage in a self-improvement program for at least six months before you expect major results, and prepare to stay involved for at least a year to two years. It takes over a year for a new habit to be imbedded strongly enough to overcome old destructive behaviors.

You have a choice of being your own worst enemy or your own best friend. Realize, once and for all, you hold the key to your personal success and happiness. You should believe that you and your children are as worthy of happiness and success as anyone. You are worthy in your own way, regardless of how you may differ from others.

And you must learn self-trust, which is the ability to feel positive, responsible, and in control of what takes place as you try to test your limits. You do this by dedicating yourself to a life-long journey of knowledge and skill development as we move through the most exciting millennium in history. By building your own healthy self-esteem you will be a worthy role model, coach, and leader, to set the example for everyone in your personal and professional life, especially your own children.

Here are some action reminders to help you develop a more positive self-esteem:

1. Dress and look your best at all times, regardless of the pressure from your friends and peers. Personal grooming and appearance provide an instantaneous projection on the surface of how you feel inside about yourself. You don't have to be the best-looking in any group, just look your best. Being clean says you care about yourself. Make a commitment to join a support group with a proven program that will overcome any habit that reduces the quality of your life.

2. Improve your body language. Stand erect yet relaxed. Walk purposefully but without arrogance. Your jaw and face should be relaxed, your eyes bright and in direct contact with others while in conversation, your pronunciation should be clear, and

your voice projecting confidence and intensity. Always extend your hand and offer your own name first in any personal encounter, and offer your name first in phone conversations. Smile with your eyes, voice, face, and body language. In virtually every culture, a smile is a light in your window that says a caring person resides within.

3. Dwell on your strengths and talents. Keep a video webpage or Facebook record of your professional and personal milestones and achievements—positive memories for reinforcement during difficult times. Also, make a video of the older members of your family and senior members of your company relating their experiences and their expertise. Nothing is more important to rookies and the younger generation than wisdom from people who have been there before. And nothing is more important than featuring dedicated employees who may not be getting the attention they deserve.

4. Make the first and last fifteen minutes of your day at home and at the office—the time we call sign-on and sign-off signatures—the most important for all around you. Make it a habit, no less important than brushing your teeth, to start your day on a positive note. Wake up looking forward to a new slate. Send your partner or spouse off with a loving, encouraging thought. Send yourself off to work with a bright outlook. Send everyone at your factory or office forward with the expected results, not the morning newspaper's bad news.

Just as important, use the last fifteen minutes of your office and family day to let others know how much you care for them—by signing off with a reassuring, optimistic sentence or two. Just before leaving the office, think of something in your working environment that brings you satisfaction and pass it on. Do the same at home before going to sleep. We believe this has influenced our family to rise higher in their aspirations. We know it has changed our own lives.

Questions: In your journal or a place you can refer to, make a simple list of what is in your BAG: B—Blessings? What blessings do you take for granted? A—Accomplishments? What you are proud of? G—Goals? What are you reaching for? By dwelling on the answers to those few questions, you will never want to trade "bags" with anyone else.

Action: When anyone pays you a compliment for any reason, reply with a warm "thank you," and return the compliment in some way. This is the best way to pay value forward.

The most important three words you can say to yourself: Yes, I can!

Character cannot be counterfeited or created by the media. Like rings within a tree, we become what we do.

Chapter 3

The Trust Factor–Integrity:
The Real Bottom Line

SINCERITY: LIVING WITHOUT WAX

elf-honesty is the ability to step back from the canvas of life and take a good look at yourself as you relate to your environmental, physical, mental, and spiritual world. Self-honesty is the ability to accept yourself as a unique, imperfect, changing, and growing individual and to recognize your own vast potential as well as your limitations. Self-honesty is the ability to separate prejudice from truth, which is so challenging because each of us looks at life through a filter of past experience and ingrained beliefs.

A simple motto hung on the living room wall of my grandparents' small frame house, where many seeds for my development were planted. My grandmother and grandfather didn't talk about the lines; they lived them. "Life is like a field of newly fallen snow; where I choose to walk, every step will show." They believed you were either honest or you weren't. There was nothing in between, no such thing as partial honesty. Integrity, a standard of personal morality and ethics, is not relative to the situation you happen to find yourself in and doesn't sell out to expediency. Its short supply is getting even shorter—but without it, leadership is a facade. People unconcerned with self-respect and able to see little value in themselves will not guide their lives with such an internal compass. Unfortunately, their own inner value system is thoroughly mixed up, even inverted. I find real confusion about self-respect among the current and younger generations, whose comments seem to indicate that they take braggarts, clowns, and celebrities as role models—people who appear successful but are often submerged in show. "Can you believe he/she actually spoke to me?" I often hear students saying about stars. That's not entirely their fault; our society puts a huge premium on celebrity for celebrity's sake. Even politicians running for the highest offices in the nation are elected more on star status than leadership qualities, much as high school students might select the king and queen of the senior prom.

Learning to see through exteriors is a critical development in the transition from adolescence to adulthood. Sadly, most people continue to be taken in by big talk and media popularity, flashy or bizarre looks, and expensive possessions. They move through most of their years convinced that the externals are what count and are thus doomed to live shallow lives. Those who rely on their looks or status to feel good about themselves inevitably do everything they can to enhance the impression they make—and do correspondingly little to develop their inner value and personal growth. The paradox is that the people who try hardest to impress are often the least impressive. Devotion to image is often for the money and influence it can reap.

Puffing to appear powerful is an attempt to hide insecurity. If only we could see many of our celebrities when their guard and pretenses were down!

An essay in *Time* magazine tackled one of our culture's great problems: the tabloid celebration of the famous and the infamous. Any moral crusade will run smack into the messages conveyed by our growing celebrity-obsessed culture. A few moments in the limelight can mean big bucks: a book contract, a speaking tour, a TV docudrama, or a reality show. Ethical distinctions are quickly lost as talk-show appearances and gala opening-night parties become schools for scandal. The myth that all that counts is bottom-line success often leads to fleeting stardom and ultimate defeat. Ask a thousand has-beens.

In the Roman Empire's final corrupt years, status was conveyed by the number of carved statues of the gods displayed in people's courtyards. As in every business, the Roman statue industry had good and bad sculptors and merchants. As the empire became ever more greedy and narcissistic, the bad got away with as much as they could. Sculptors became so adept at using wax to hide cracks and chips in marble that most people couldn't discern the difference in quality. Statues began to weep or melt under the scrutiny of sunlight or heat in foyers. For statues of authentic fine quality, carved by reputable artists, people had to go to the artisan marketplace in the Roman Quad and look for booths with signs declaring *sine cera* (without wax). We too look for the real thing in friends, products, and services. In people, we value sincerity—from *sine cera*—more than almost any other virtue. We should expect it from our leaders. We must demand it of ourselves.

Self-honesty is the foundation of self-knowledge. In order to improve yourself, it is important to be able to see yourself accurately, without being too harsh or too generous. Ask yourself, "Am I seeing myself as I really am? Am I overconfident, or am I selling myself short?"

Self-honesty requires effort. It involves telling the truth about yourself, both to yourself and to others. Telling the truth about yourself means admitting that you are human and therefore imperfect. Being honest can be challenging, because it involves revealing thoughts and feelings that we might dislike and that might not fit in with our self-image. Self-honesty entails confronting aspects of your past and present that are unpleasant or even painful. It might even involve confronting painful feelings such as sadness, grief, anger, fear, shame, or guilt.

The benefits of self-honesty far outweigh the effort it requires. With self-honesty, you can see both what you have to offer and what you need to do to become the person you want to be. When you are honest with yourself, you are able to take pride in your progress because you know that you have set meaningful goals and invested the effort necessary to reach them. Who you are, what you think, and how you feel are all in harmony.

To become more self-honest, try to look at yourself like an archaeologist at the site of an exciting, newly discovered city. An archaeologist doesn't judge what he or she finds but tries to understand it. In the same way, don't look for what "should" be—look for what "is." Take inventory of everything you find— the precious treasures of current and future potential and joy, and the learning experiences from the past.

What can we do to increase the dwindling integrity in our society today? Like charity, integrity begins at home. One of the greatest gifts you can give your children is a strong sense of ethical and moral values. Let them accept responsibility for their own actions as early as possible. The more sense of responsibility they develop, the better they will feel about themselves. Above all, for integrity's sake, teach them graciousness and gratitude and how to care about the rights and welfare of others. Teach your children (and business associates who look to you for leadership) that their true rewards in life will depend on the quality and amount of service they render. Show them, by example, how to treat others as they would have others treat them. As the grandfather of 11 grandchildren, I know from experience that the greatest gifts parents can give their children—and that business and other leaders can give their team members—are roots and wings. Roots lie in core values and feelings of self-worth. Wings grow from acceptance of responsibility, which enables our children to fly freely as independent adults. The loss of roots and wings too often leads to pursuit of "loot and things" and other tragic results.

Being honest with yourself and others is one of the key ingredients in authentic success over a lifetime. Mutual trust is the glue that binds all relationships. Self-honesty is the ability to separate prejudice from truth, which is so challenging because each of us looks at life through a filter of past experience and ingrained beliefs. Integrity is easier preached than practiced. We go along for a while setting a good example, but sometimes we tell ourselves we need a break. Our children and team members get confused. First they think we are being ourselves by modeling healthy behavior. When they see unhealthy behavior coming from their leaders, they are puzzled and hurt at first, but then they catch on. They learn to play the game of "say one thing" and do "something different." The old cliché holds true: What you are speaks so loudly no one can really hear what you say. But it is even more true that if what you think, say, and do are consistent, your life will speak forcefully indeed.

Your children—and those you work with who look to you for leadership—will do what they see you do. Your challenge as a leader is enormous, but so are the rewards. A life of principle—of not succumbing to the temptations of easy morality—will always win in the end, leading you to the real wealth of a clear conscience and not having to constantly check the rear-view mirror as you move forward.

IT'S NOT OK, JUST BECAUSE EVERYBODY DOES IT

The following anecdote—extracted from an article appearing in *The Chicago Sun-Times*—illustrates graphically what we are talking about. It's powerful stuff and it's titled:

"It's O.K. Son, Everybody Does It."

When Johnny was six years old, he was with his father riding in his car and his father was pulled over for speeding. His father handed the officer a volunteer-sheriff's badge, and a $100 bill for a donation, along with his driver's license. As they drove off without a citation, the father told him: "It's OK, son, everybody does it."

When he was eight, he was at a family meeting presided over by Uncle George, on the surest means to shave points off your income tax return. "It's OK, kid," his uncle said. "Everybody does it." When he was nine, his mother took him to his first theater production. The person in the box office couldn't find decent seats until his mother discovered an extra twenty dollars in her purse. "It's OK, son," she said, "everybody does it.

When he was eleven, his aunt helped him get an additional "free" pair of prescription eyeglasses by filing an insurance claim that his first pair had been lost or stolen. "It's OK, Johnny," his aunt said, "everybody does it."

When he was fifteen, he made first-string right guard on the high school football team. His coach showed him how to block and, at the same time, grab the opposing end by the jersey so the officials couldn't see it. "It's, OK, kid," the coach said, "everybody does it."

When he was sixteen, he took his first summer job at the supermarket. His assignment was to put the overripe strawberries in the bottom of the boxes and the good ones on top where they would show. "It's OK, kid," the manager said, "everybody does it." When he was eighteen, Johnny and a friend applied for a college scholarship. Johnny was a marginal student. His buddy was in the upper three percent of his class, but he couldn't play right guard. Johnny got the scholarship. "It's OK, son," his parents assured him. "Everybody does it."

When he was nineteen, he was approached by an upperclassman who offered him the test answers for fifty dollars. "It's OK, kid. Everybody does it." Johnny was caught and sent home in disgrace. "How could you do this to your mother and me?" his father vented. "You never learned anything like this at home." His aunt and uncle were also shocked. If there's one thing the adult world can't stand, it's a kid who cheats.

That message has the same impact as Harry Chapin's classic song, "The Cat's in the Cradle," which ends with the poignant lines: "And when I hung up the phone it occurred to me, my son was just like me. Yeah. He grew up, just like me."

If I were writing a single commandment for leadership, it would be: "You shall conduct yourself in such a manner as to set an example worthy of imitation by your children and subordinates." In simpler terms, if they shouldn't be doing it, neither should you.

When I told my kids to clean their rooms, for example, they took a closer look at the condition of my tools and possessions in the garage. When I told them that honesty was our family's greatest virtue, they commented on the radar detector I had installed in my car. When I told them about the vices of drinking and wild parties, they watched from the upstairs balcony the way our guests behaved at our adult functions.

It's hardly a secret that learning ethical standards begins at home. A child's first inklings of a sense of right and wrong come from almost imperceptible signals received long before he or she reaches the age of rational thought about morality. Maybe you're asking yourself what kind of model you are for future generations, remembering that people are either honest or dishonest, that integrity is all or nothing, and that children can't be fooled in such basic matters. They learn by example.

I'd rather watch a winner than hear one any day.

So please, my loving parents, let your lives show me the way.

I'm only a reflection of what you taught today.

I may misunderstand you and the high advice you give,

But there's no misunderstanding how you act and how you live.

So teach me by example, don't preach about what's right

And show me by your actions every day and night.

I know that you're not perfect in the things you do and say

And the lectures you deliver are to help me find my way.

But I'd rather watch a winner than hear one any day.

Questions: If everyone in your family, team, or organization had your integrity, what kind of family, team, or organization would it be? What do you think about expecting leaders to be honest in their personal lives, as well as in their professional positions? Is there a difference?

Action: Before you share something you read on the Internet, check the source to determine if it is "authentic from a reputable source" or "an opinion or infomercial for a product, service, or political belief."

THE INTEGRITY TRIAD

Stand up for truth under pressure. Give others the credit when due. Be real and genuine.

One of the principles of integrity is to defend your convictions in the face of great social pressure. Consider this true story about an abdominal surgery performed in a large, well-known hospital. It was the surgical nurse's first day on the medical team. Responsible for ensuring that all instruments and materials were accounted for before completing the operation and sewing up the incision, she told the surgeon that he had removed only eleven sponges. "We used twelve and we need to find the last one," she reported. "No, I removed them all," the doctor declared emphatically. "We'll close the incision now." "No," the rookie nurse objected, "we used twelve sponges." "I'll take the responsibility," the surgeon said grimly. "Suture, please." "You can't do that, sir," blazed the nurse. "Think of the patient!" The surgeon lifted his foot, revealing where he had hidden the twelfth sponge. "You'll do just fine in this or any other hospital," he said, smiling. Integrity principle one: Don't back down when you know you're right.

A second, key integrity principle is always to give others the credit that's rightfully theirs, never fearing anyone who has a better idea or is smarter than you. David Ogilvy, founder of Ogilvy and Mather, made this point to newly appointed office heads by sending each of them a matryoshka, the painted Russian doll with five progressively smaller dolls nestled inside. His message to his new executives was in the smallest doll: "If we hire people who are smaller than we are, we'll become a company of dwarves. But if each of us hires people bigger than we are, we'll become a company of giants." And that is precisely what Ogilvy and Mather became, one of the world's largest and most respected advertising firms.

Our third integrity principle is to be honest and open about who you really are. Be genuine. Don't exaggerate your achievements. Don't get trapped in a cover-up of past mistakes, even of personal traits that dissatisfy or displease you. When the going is tough, be tough by facing reality with adult responses. Use the good and the bad as material for personal growth. We must teach our children, and others who look to us for leadership, self-respect, and the supreme value of a clean conscience as early as possible. They are powerful components of integrity. Integrity that strengthens an inner value system is the real human bottom line. Commitment to a life of integrity in every situation demonstrates that your word is more valuable than a surety bond. It means you don't base your decisions on being politically correct. You do what's right, not what's fashionable. You know that truth is absolute, not a device for manipulating others. And you win in the long run, when the stakes are highest.

I love discussing integrity with high school students. I throw a wallet into the center of the room where we—members of a small seminar—are sitting in a circle. The wallet contains a driver's license, credit cards, photos, and eight $100 bills. I ask the students one by one what they would do if they found the wallet on a deserted street. The answers are uncomfortably revealing. "Wow, that would be awesome!" goes the most typical. "I'd keep the money as my reward and mail back the wallet with the credit cards." Other students invariably suggest not putting a return address on the envelope so the owner couldn't call and ask if there was money in the wallet when it was found. I usually ask how the $800 windfall would be explained to parents and friends. And if word got around—and ultimately back to the owner—would they say, "Losers weepers, finders keepers"?

Then I place the wallet in special situational contexts. What if the driver's license showed that the wallet belonged to your best friend? Or to your mother? What if you recognized the driver's license photograph as that of an elderly neighbor who lived on Social Security and who probably dropped the wallet on her way to the hospital for kidney dialysis, which she needed every week? Most students somberly agree that in those specific situations, it would be best to return the money, too. (One once ventured a slight exception if the wallet belonged to his mother: She'd understand, he assured us, if a few hundred dollars were missing.)

Finally, I ask an even more sensitive—and defining—question: "What if you were at an airport ready to fly off on a student summer tour of Hawaii or Australia. You use the restroom and leave your wallet—containing eight $100 bills—on the sink when you wash your hands. Realizing what you're missing as you board the plane, you run back, explain your emergency to the gate agent and race to the restroom, heart pounding. If you were in that situation, what would you hope?"

"That the wallet's on the sink where I left it," most call out in unison. "And what do you hope is in the wallet?" I continue.

"Eight $100 bills and my credit cards and my driver's license," they chorus. "And if a good Samaritan like you has picked up your wallet, what do you hope he or she does?" "Turns it into lost and found or airport security or a gate agent," they say—with all the money intact. From there, we return to the wallet found on the deserted street. Now the students, many with wisdom-widened eyes, are clear about treating it as they'd want others to behave if the wallet belonged to them. The point has been made. Honesty and integrity are non-situational—and inner standards for your performance and behavior are the foundation of true self-respect.

Question: Would you say that others consider you "sincere" and trustworthy?

Action: When you disagree with someone important to you, be able to say, "I understand why you take the position you do; however, I would like to share with you why I feel differently!"

SITUATIONAL INTEGRITY: A NEW OXYMORON

Specific situations require different management approaches and styles—but how do you feel about the term situational integrity? We've seen that if integrity applies only in specific situations, it's not integrity at all but expediency. Do you believe in absolutes or does everything derive from your point of view, your (temporary) advantage? To answer that question with another question, you might ask what your family or your company or our world would be like if everyone had your ethics. The choice is yours. We'd either be in terrific or terrible shape. Of course people do cheat to get ahead; you know that. But when you maintain your integrity at all costs, even if you feel you might suffer in the short term, you'll win hands down in the end.

Most importantly, you'll be an inner winner, with victories no one can ever take from you. Is stealing paper clips, note pads, and rubber bands from your office anything to worry about? A person of integrity is not tempted down that slippery slope that can lead to more serious situations, even embezzlement. Is integrity a primary consideration in a practical, profit-making organization? Not to have it courts the risk of sophisticated surveillance equipment, disgruntled employees, and whistle blowers. Ethics deprivation can lead to inner rot. The company building may be located in a high-rent district. It may be made of the finest steel, chrome, and glass—but it will decay from the inside.

Can you think of a successful relationship without integrity? I doubt it. All are based on mutual trust. Break that trust and you break the relationship. Subvert it and it's almost impossible to put together again. Creating a long-term relationship takes two or more people—whether executives, representatives of labor and management, or husband and wife who are grounded in and operating on the same non-situational integrity. Nothing less will last.

When *Fortune* magazine asked the CEOs of many Fortune 500 companies what they considered the most important qualities for hiring and promoting top executives, the unanimous consensus was that integrity and trustworthiness were by far the key qualities. That survey of leading businessmen—not of preachers or motivational speakers—speaks for itself.

Here are some tips to help you further embrace integrity in your personal, business, and family life:

1. Justice and fair play are integrity's core values. Go out of your way to be helpful and make others Number One in your life. A smile will almost always be returned with a smile—and you're none the worse for wear even if it's not.

2. Set high standards of ethics for yourself and expect others to do the same. Your single most powerful teaching tool is not talking about what's right but quietly doing it. A businessperson or a parent who lectures about obeying the rules but constantly breaks them is making an especially powerful negative statement. The old "Do as I say, not as I do" is severely damaging to children and subordinates.

3. Give of your best in the worst of times. Personal integrity knows no season and doesn't hinge on the weather, the stock market report, or the leading economic indicators. You have it or you don't.

4. Respect diversity in culture and heritage. The world's rapid transportation, interactive media, virtual reality, and global communications network

means we must learn to live in harmony with other human beings. The dictionary tells us that integrity is wholeness, which implies mutual acceptance. Don't make the futile attempt of trying to be an island. Welcome the foreigner. Work hard at understanding other cultures, languages, and points of view.

Your children and subordinates will do what they see you do. Your job as a leader is enormous, but so are the rewards. A life of principle—of not succumbing to the temptations of easy morality—will always win in the end, leading you to the real wealth of the 21st century.

Question: Do you interpret "diversity" as something you see immediately with your eyes? Or do you look at diversity as the richness in heritage, culture, and experience of those with backgrounds different from your own?

Action: Reach out to someone today who is being excluded from your circle of colleagues or friends because of their apparent differences. Seek to include him or her.

Be a role model, not a critic.

Losers let it happen;
winners make it happen!

Chapter 4

Living by Choice:
Responsibility for Outcomes

THE LAW OF CAUSE AND EFFECT

Winners take full responsibility for determining their actions in their own lives. They believe in cause and effect and have the philosophy that life is a "do-it-to-yourself" program. Many people refuse to face the truth in the mirror of their lives on a daily basis and prefer to hide behind the belief that fate, luck, or possibly their astrological sign have shaped the outcome of their lives. These people who feel that life is mostly determined by circumstances, predestination, or being at the right place at the right time are more likely to give in to doubt and fear. Those who cannot make up their minds for fear of making the wrong choice, vacillating in indecision, simply do not achieve their goals—a requisite for success. Rather, they take their place among the rank and file, trudging along in mediocrity.

In his classic book, *Self-Renewal*, John Gardner states that winning individuals do not leave the development of their potential to chance. They pursue it honestly, systematically, and look forward to an endless dialogue between their potentials and the claims of life—not only the claims they encounter, but the claims they invent. Daily, thousands of individuals are finding that there is a bright new world out there to be discovered and are demonstrating Gardner's statement that "we don't know we've been imprisoned until we've broken out."

People who are aware that they exert control over what happens to them in life are happier and are able to choose more appropriate responses to whatever occurs. All individuals are what they are and where they are as a composite result of all their own doings. Although our innate characteristics and environment are given to us initially, the decisions we make determine whether we win or lose our particular game of life.

Voltaire likened life to a game of cards. Each player must accept the cards life deals him or her. But once they are in hand, he or she alone must decide how to play the cards in order to win the game. The writer, John Erskine, put it a little differently when he wrote: "Though we sometimes speak of a primrose path, we all know that a bad life is just as difficult, just as full of work, obstacles, and hardships, as a good one. The only choice is the kind of life one would care to spend one's efforts on."

I had the good fortune to learn about self-reliance early in life. My father had gone overseas in World War II. I was nine and the eldest boy in the family, so I spent most of my time helping my mother make ends meet and taking care of my younger siblings. There was an army antiaircraft gun emplacement near our home in San Diego, California. The soldiers stationed there would make friends with us to occupy their lonely hours on duty, and they would give us military souvenirs. I received a camouflaged army helmet and a canteen for drinking water. In return, I brought them magazines and invited them over for some home cooking, such as it was. We had little money and couldn't afford much food, and I learned later that the soldiers were more interested in my sister than they were in me.

I'll never forget the evening when one of those soldier friends said, "I want to take you fishing in a boat, Sunday, at 5 in the morning." I replied, barely able to keep my feet on the ground, "Oh, wow, I'd love to go. I've never even been near a boat. I've always fished off the bridge, or the pier, or the rocks, and just watched the boats heading out in the ocean. But I've always dreamed of going fishing on a boat. Oh, thank you. I'll ask my mom if you can come over for dinner tomorrow."

I was so excited I went to bed with my clothes and tennis shoes on, so I'd be sure not to be late. I lay in my bed, unable to sleep, counting big sea bass and barracuda that I imagined were swimming on my ceiling. At 3 am I sneaked out of my bedroom window, got my tackle box all set with extra hooks, oiled my fishing reel, packed two peanut butter and jelly sandwiches, and at 4 am I was ready to go with my fishing pole, my tackle box, my lunch, and my enthusiasm—sitting on the curb in front of my house, waiting in the dark for my friend the soldier. But he never showed up.

That probably was a pivotal point in my young life in terms of self-reliance. Instead of crawling back to bed sulking, I went to a swap meet and spent all my lawn-mowing money on a patched-up, one-man rubber life raft. I carried it, with my gear inside, on top of my head like a safari native, all the way to the bay about a mile from my house. I pretended I was launching a cabin cruiser, as I paddled out in the bay. I caught some fish, ate my sandwiches, drank punch from my army canteen, and had one of the most marvelous days of my life. It was an all-time high.

When I look back on that day—as I often do—I always ponder what I learned. First, I learned that when the fish are biting, no problem in the world is big enough to be remembered. Second, my soldier friend taught me that having only good intentions doesn't cut it. He wanted to take me, he thought about taking me, he may even have been planning to take me before his alarm clock did or didn't go off. But, because it wasn't his burning desire or a real commitment, he didn't show. For me, however, going fishing that day was my magnificent obsession and I took action to make that obsession a reality.

Rather than live in frustration and disappointment when others don't follow through on their well-meaning promises, I try to have a contingency plan in mind so that I can keep on "doing" rather than sitting there and "stewing."

Even though I learned early lessons about self-reliance, I didn't fully realize until I was 35 that I'm behind the wheel in my life. I thought it was the government, the economy, the world situation, and my heritage. I used to think that as a Gemini, I was destined to be creative but non-specific. I should have taken a hint from one of my daughters when she was only eleven months old. She was in her highchair for dinner, and

I decided she should eat some nourishing strained squash. I tasted it to test the temperature. It was bland and not too exiting, but I knew it was good for her. I held the little curved spoon out and gently entreated, "Open up, honey, Daddy has some yummy squash for you." She stared coldly at me and clamped her mouth shut in passive defiance. Although she was unable to speak, had she been able to talk she certainly would have said, "Go ahead, Daddy, why don't you eat it." Being in total control of the situation, I simply pressed her cheeks firmly with two fingers, thus forcing her mouth open. I then neatly inserted the spoonful of squash into her mouth and quietly, but sternly, ordered, "Go on, swallow it; it's good for you." She spit it out all over my face! She had decided at eleven months old she did not like the taste of strained squash. She has grown children of her own now, who for some strange reason never liked the taste of strained squash either!

Children do begin to take control of their lives at an early age. Many children learn how to control their parents' lives as well, long before they know how to talk in complete sentences. Whining receives attention. Crying receives consolation. Begging gets goodies. Tantrums create havoc. It's easy to incite Mommy against Daddy and sit back and watch the show.

In a very real sense, we all become hostages of hundreds of restrictions of our own choosing or with the assistance of the entertainment media and our parents. As children, we either accepted or rejected the teachings and lifestyles of the significant adults in our lives. I know from experience that the greatest gifts that parents can give their children (and that managers can give their employees) are roots and wings. As we mentioned in the last chapter, roots lie in core values and feelings of self-worth. Wings grow from acceptance of responsibility, which enables our children to fly freely as independent adults. The loss of roots and wings too often leads to pursuit of "loot and things" and other tragic results.

In my parenting and leadership seminars, I tell a true story about a young couple who invited me to their home for dinner some time ago after an all-day program at a university. This man and woman, both highly intelligent with advanced degrees, had opted for a "child-centered" home so their five-year-old son, Bradford, would have everything at his disposal to become a winner out there in the competitive world. When I arrived at their driveway in front of a fashionable, two-story home, I should have known what was in store for me. I stepped on one of his many scattered toys getting out the car and was greeted by, "Watch where you're walking, Mister, or you'll have to buy me new ones!"

Entering the front door, I instantly discovered that this was Bradford's place, not his parents'! The furnishings, it appeared, were originally of fine quality before their son practiced his demolition skills on them. We attempted to have a cup of tea in the family room, but Bradford was busy ruining his new video game controls. Trying to find a place to sit down was like hopping on one foot through a minefield, blindfolded. Bradford was the first to be served with food, in the living room so that he wouldn't be lonely. I nearly dropped my hot cup in my lap in surprise when they brought out a highchair that was designed like an aircraft ejection seat with four legs and straps. He was five years old and had to be strapped in a highchair to get through one meal! (Soon, I wished it had been a real aircraft ejection seat!)

As we started our salads, young Bradford dumped his dinner on the carpet and proceeded to pour his milk on top of it to ensure that the peas and carrots would go deep into the shag fibers. His mother entreated, "Brad, honey, don't do that. Mommy wants you to grow up strong and healthy like Daddy. I'll get you some more dinner while Daddy cleans it up."

While they were occupied with their chores, Bradford had unfastened his seat belts, scrambled down from his perch, and joined me in the dining room, helping himself to my olives. "I think you should wait for your own dinner," I said politely, removing his hand from my salad bowl. He swung his leg up to kick me in the knee, but my old ex-pilot reflexes didn't fail me, and I crossed my legs so quickly that he missed, came off his feet and came down hard on the floor on the seat of his pants. You'd have thought he was at the dentist's office. He screamed and ran to his mother, sobbing, "He hit me!" When his parents asked what happened, I calmly informed them that he had fallen accidentally and that, besides, "I'd never hit the head of a household!"

I knew it was time to be on my way when they put their little prince to bed by placing granola cookies on the stairs as enticers. And he ate his way up to bed! "How are you ever going to motivate him to go to school?" I asked quietly. "Oh, I'm sure we'll come up with something," they laughed. "Yes, but what if the neighborhood dogs eat what you put out? He'll lose his way just like Hansel and Gretel!" The couple didn't find that humorous and never invited me back.

As a traveling lecturer, I see many children throughout the world who are in charge of their parents. I also observe many teenagers and adults who, as a result of overly permissive or overly strict leadership at home, are out of control. Life's greatest risk is being spoiled or pampered and then feeling entitled to depend on others for your security, which can really come only by planning, acting, and making choices that will make you independent. Leadership ideas that solve problems and create opportunity come from creative trial-and-error thinking.

Years of study and some painful personal experiences have convinced us that fear of the costs of success are among the reasons prejudiced people resist change. For success does have its price, including:

Taking responsibility for giving up bad habits and invalid assumptions.

Taking responsibility for setting an example in our own lives.

Distancing ourselves from a peer group that isn't helping us succeed and therefore tends or wants to hold us back.

Leading ourselves and others down a new and unfamiliar path.

Working more to reach a goal and being willing to delay gratifications along the way.

Being willing to face criticism and jealousy from people who would like to keep us stuck in place with them.

These are among the perceived costs of success that prompt people to escape from the present by occupying their minds with past memories or future expectations. Leaders, by contrast, are not dismayed by the cost of success. They get started and build positive momentum. Determined to pursue their potential, they look forward to an endless dialogue between their talents and the claims of life.

Winners live by making choices, rather than taking chances. It's true that things turn out best for people who make the best out of whatever comes up on a daily basis. Although our innate characteristics and environment are given to us initially, the decisions we make determine whether we win or lose our particular game of life. We in the developed nations, with access to knowledge and communication, are fortunate to be more in control of our destinies than those in the most impoverished areas of the world in which just having food and water for the week are the primary goals and challenges.

I still continue to experience parents who feel so guilty about the lack of quality and quantity of time they spend with their children that they spoil their kids by overindulging them into feeling like entitled little emperors and empresses. When kids feel entitled, they don't feel responsible for paying the price of success. They grow up as whiners who remain dependent on others for their outcomes.

What you make of your life is up to you. You have all the tools and resources you need. What you do with them is your decision. The choice is yours, and it's never too late to get in the game.

Consider Sister Mary Martin Weaver, a Catholic nun, who took up athletics many years ago—at the age of fifty-five. She has won forty-four gold, silver, and bronze medals in a variety of events, including the five-thousand-meter race walk, snow-shoe racing, speed and figure skating, basketball free throws, shot put, and ice hockey!

At an age when most people are going for the gold medal in napping, Sister Mary has become a fixture at the U.S. National Senior Olympics. "People have gotten flabby," she says, "and I don't mean just physically. Anything that requires real effort, they just don't want to do. But there are no rewards in anything unless you try. Age should never be a barrier to full participation in life. What's most important is to enjoy life to its fullest, to do things for and with others, and never, ever be afraid to stretch your limits. Choose to win!"

Many people engage in pleasurable activities with no particular result in mind. We call this immediate gratification. Winners choose activities that will give them long-term positive results as well as daily satisfaction. That's delayed gratification.

I had the good fortune to work with one of America's best NFL football teams, the Chicago Bears, who won the Superbowl in 1985. I became a friend and colleague of one of the greatest running backs in the history of American football, who is one of the leading ground-gainers of all time. There's a steep hill in a suburb of Chicago that played a significant role in the making of this champion.

During the off-season, every off-season, he would run up that steep hill every day. No matter how hot and humid the day might get, regardless of thunderstorms or mud, he still charged up that hill over and over again. Sometimes other players would join him, even players from other teams throughout the league would race him. After a short time they all would quit, totally exhausted. They couldn't believe anyone would be that obsessed with conquering a hill. But he urged them to keep going until they dropped, and even then, he went a few more times. Finally, when he felt he too had enough, he went one last time.

When football season came again, he fought for every yard, every inch. It usually took more than one opponent to bring him down. And near the end of the games, when victory or defeat was still undecided, that hill would really pay off for Walter Payton of the Chicago Bears. While others faded, he would seem to get stronger. That he was talented is without question. But all professional players have talent. What Payton also had was that hill. It wasn't fun. It wasn't glamorous. It wasn't publicized by the media. It was, quite simply, his way of paying the price for success.

When you, like Sister Mary and Walter Payton, have paid the price in full, you too can have the best seat in the house. The one at the top of the hill. Winners live by making choices, rather than taking chances. In the previous chapter, we focused on the fact that people who are aware that they exert control over what happens to them in life are happier and are able to choose more appropriate responses to whatever occurs. It's true that things turn out best for people who make the best out of whatever comes up on a daily basis. Although our innate characteristics and environment are given to us initially, the decisions we make determine whether we win or lose our particular game of life. We in the developed nations, with access to knowledge and communication, are fortunate to be more in control of our destinies than those in the most impoverished areas of the world in which just having food and water for the week are the primary goals and challenges.

Questions: What kind of pressure do you feel to conform to the standards, views, and beliefs of your peer group? Can you fit in and stand out at the same time?

Action: Be aware today that others may try to hold you back with them, rather than want you to move ahead. Take more responsibility for your outcomes today by being proactive, instead of reactive. Be different if it means to care more, do more, give more, and expect more. Ask for or assume more responsibility today.

WHO IS IN CHARGE?

Just as companies must dissolve their boundaries and erase their hierarchies, so must you, the individual, reinvent yourself to meet the knowledge era's changing demands. What this means is that you're your own chief executive officer. Start thinking of yourself as a service company with a single employee. You're a small company—very small, but that doesn't matter—that puts your services to work for a larger company. Tomorrow you may sell those services to a different organization, but that doesn't mean you're any less loyal to your current employer.

The first step is resolving not to suffer the fate of those who lost their jobs and found their skills were obsolete. The second is to begin immediately the process of protecting yourself against that possibility—by becoming proactive instead of reactive.

Ask yourself how vulnerable you are and what you can do about it. "What trends must I watch? What information must I gain? What knowledge do I lack?" Again, think of yourself as a company—for this purpose a research and development company—and establish your own strategic planning department. Set up a training department and make sure your top employee is updating his or her skills. Start your own investment plan, knowing that you are responsible for your own financial security.

You're your own CEO who must have the vision to set your goals and allocate your resources. Since your primary concern is ensuring your viability in the marketplace, you must think strategically in every decision. This mindset of being responsible for your own future used to be crucial only to the self-employed, but it has become essential for us all. For today's typical workers are no longer one-career people. Most will have several separate careers in their lifetimes. But although you must become your own life's CEO and always act as if you were a company of one, being a team leader is equally important for your future. It's no longer possible to achieve alone in our world of accelerating change, where the new global village has become the local neighborhood. Rather than become dependent on others, however, we should become interdependent, treating everyone we meet as a potential customer, someone with whom we may develop a strategic alliance in the future.

Although many things in life are beyond anyone's control, you do have a great deal of control—more than most of us are willing to acknowledge—over many circumstances and conditions. Here are what I refer to as the Seven C's of Control that I consider most important:

1. You can control what you do with most of your free time during the day and the evening.

2. You can control your concepts and imagination, channel what you think about.

3. You can control who you choose as role models and who you'll seek out for mentoring counsel and inspiration. You can control who you spend your leisure time with—and, to a great degree, with whom you communicate.

4. You can control your tongue; you can choose to remain silent or choose to speak. If you choose to speak, you can choose your words and your tone of voice.

5. You can control the causes to which you give your time and goals. This is what we call the purpose behind the purpose.

6. You can control your commitments, the things you absolutely promise yourself and others that you'll do.

7. You can control your concerns and worries—and whether you'll choose to take action about them, as well as your response to difficult times and people.

As I approach the winter of my life, I choose my battles carefully and spend my precious time planting shade trees for future generations, under which I, myself will never sit. Time has become my most precious resource. I am devoted to living life as if every moment were part of Prime Time.

Prime time, to most people, is that period between 6 and 10 p.m. during which most of the general public watches television. Commercials in prime time are the most expensive, approaching much more than a million dollars per minute. My real success in life took a quantum leap when I stopped watching other people making money in their professions—performing in prime time—and started living my own dreams and goals in prime time. Of all the wisdom I have gained over my 50-plus-year career, the knowledge that time and health are taken for granted until they are depleted has caused me to reorder my daily priorities. As with health, time is the raw material of life. We can bide our time, but we can't save it for another day. We can waste and kill time, but we are also mortally wounding our opportunities.

Time is the ultimate equal-opportunity employer. Each human being has exactly 168 hours a week to spend. Think about it! Scientists can't invent more minutes. Super-rich people can't buy more hours. Queen Elizabeth the First of England—the richest, most powerful woman on earth of her era—whispered these final words on her deathbed: "All of my possessions for another moment of time!"

We worry about things we want to do but can't, instead of doing the things we can do but don't. It is not the experience of today that causes us the greatest stress. It is the regret for something we did or didn't do yesterday and the apprehension of what tomorrow may bring. Time never stops to rest, never hesitates, never looks forward or backward. Life's raw material spends itself in the now, this moment, which is why how you spend your time is far more important than all the material possessions you may own or positions you may obtain. Positions change, possessions come and go, and you can earn more money. You can renew your supply of many things, but like good health, that other most precious resource, time spent is gone forever.

Each yesterday, and all of them together, are beyond your control. Literally all the money in the world can't undo or redo a single act you performed. You cannot erase a single word you said, can't add an "I love you," "I'm sorry," or "I forgive you," not even a "thank you" you forgot to say.

Consider this: Most of your daytime hours are spent helping other people solve their problems. The little time you have in the evenings and on weekends is all you have to spend on yourself, on your own dreams and goals, and personal development. To me, that's why I prefer to live in Prime Time rather than watch TV in Prime Time.

Have dinner with your loved ones at least two to three times per week. It's the best time for casual conversation to listen to what those close to you feel is important in their lives. Mealtime is a time to dialogue. Record the shows that interfere with supper together. Make dinner time, family, and significant others' intimate networking time.

A television set is an appliance. It should be used, at most, for two hours at a time. It should be off, unless specific programs of interest are selected. It should not be used as a one-eyed babysitter. For the most part, TV exposes us to negative role models and serves as a tension-relieving, rather than a goal-achieving, tool. The same is true with computers, tablets, and smartphones. They, also, are wonderful tools. But they are appliances. They can become a virtual world in which we live, keeping us from exploring the natural world in person.

Instead of watching television, why not read a good fiction or non-fiction book; engage in a hobby or craft; spend time with loved ones; visit a friend or someone in need of encouragement; go out to an ethnic restaurant, a home show, an entrepreneurial show, a musical recital, a play, a fitness class, or cultural event. Take an art or photography class.

Use prime time to live the kind of life others put on layaway. As for me, I'm tired of watching life go by as a spectator doing the wave in the stands. In turning off the TV, I'm able to turn on to actual experiences I can touch, feel, smell, and in which I can engage all my senses. Instead of virtual reality, I want the real thing. An action step which fits into the concept of living in "prime time" is to balance your workload with a generous number of what I call mini-vacations for maximum productivity.

By re-energizing and renewing yourself frequently, you will avoid burnout and become much more motivated and productive. Don't keep your nose to the grindstone for years and wait for retirement to travel. In an uncertain global economy, retirement may be delayed or not considered at all. You may even want to come out of retirement and "retry" yourself in another profession or home business. Balance and consistency are the keys. Enjoy the process, not just the result. Don't fight the passing of time. Don't fear it, chase it, squander it, or try to hide from it under a superficial cosmetic veil of fads and indulgences. Life and time go together.

It's not in the image of our big dreams that we run the risk of losing our focus and motivation. It's the drudgery and routine of our daily lives that present the greatest danger to our hopes for achievement. Good time management means that you maximize the daily return on the energy and mental effort you expend. Here are some ways to maximize your time: Write down in one place all the important contacts you have and all of your goals and priorities. Make a back-up copy, preferably on a cloud platform. Write down every commitment you make at the time you make it.

Stop wasting the first hour of your workday. Having the chat and first cup of coffee, reading the paper, texting, tweeting, and socializing are costly opening exercises that lower productivity. Do one thing well at a time. It takes time to start and stop work on each activity. Stay with a task until it is completed. Don't open unimportant mail. More than a fourth of the mail you receive can be tossed before you open or read it, and that includes e-mail.

Spend twenty minutes at the beginning of each week and ten minutes at the beginning of each day planning your to-do list. Set aside personal relaxation time during the day. Don't work during lunch. It's neither noble nor nutritional to skip important energy input and stress-relieving time. Throughout the day, ask yourself, "What's the best use of my time right now?" As the day grows short, focus on projects you can least afford to leave undone.

And take vacations often, mini-vacations of two or three days, and leave your work at home. The harder you work, the more you need to balance your exercise and leisure time. Make the time of your life *Prime Time!*

Question: What do you control and what is out of your control in your daily life?

Action: For the next week, resist watching TV in prime time, which is when all the reality shows, docudramas, and sitcoms are playing each evening. Instead of watching actors and icons making money and having fun in their professions, do something active that improves your life. Family, reading, art, music, writing, recreation, service, playing games. Anything that is "doing," instead of "viewing."

RESPONSIBILITY IN ACTION

My friend and colleague, the late Stephen Covey, defined responsibility in his own way: "Look at the word responsibility as two words: response and ability—the ability to choose your response," wrote Stephen in his best-selling *The Seven Habits of Highly Effective People*. "Highly proactive people recognize and embrace responsibility. They do not blame circumstances, conditions, or conditioning for their behavior. Their behavior is a product of their own conscious choice based on values, rather than a product of their conditions, based on feeling."

Everyone likes to talk about freedom of choice. After all, that's one of the principles on which democratic nations are founded. But we often tend to feel that much of what we must do in life has been forced on us. Is that true? Must you go to work, for example? The ultimate answer is no. You can choose to lie in bed, fake an illness, move in with someone willing to support you, or apply for long-term government assistance. Must you pay taxes? Not really. You can earn too little to qualify, try to fool the government tax office, give up your citizenship, go to prison, or invest in tax-deferral programs that last until your death—after which your heirs can pay your taxes. You have to work late tonight? Not exactly. You don't have to. Many people feel compelled to work late at the office. However, those who understand positive self-determination choose to do that occasionally because they feel they have commitments that require important things to be accomplished. Leaders realize that working forty hours a week is usually enough to make a living—and also understand that their success depends on a good deal more.

We really don't have to do much of anything. We choose to do the things we do because they're profitable to us and the best choice among the alternatives. People who feel they must do things usually forfeit many available options and alternatives, losing control of their lives in the bargain. But those who are aware that they have the power of decision—that they exert control over what happens to them—can choose more effective responses to change and to life's offerings. (Note the word response again.) Incidentally, the second category of people is also generally happier.

Unfortunately, we're living in an age of eroding responsibility. Although most people are willing to fight for the credit when good things happen, fewer and fewer want to accept responsibility for their own actions. The "Why me?" so often heard today should be "Try me!" "Try me, I can handle it." "Give me the chance, and I'll do the job." Blaming others—parents, bosses, companies, immigrants, fate, weather, bad luck, the government, or the horoscope—is a mark of a juvenile mind. The mature mind asks what is within me that caused this to happen. "What did I fail to consider? What can I do better next time?" Instead of contemplating what's ticking inside them, blame-fixers focus on what's going on around them. It's always easier to assume the faults lie elsewhere.

Rather than remorse and apology or determination to face the consequences, the common response to lapses and failures is to blame one's upbringing or other circumstances. Today's philosophy often seems to be, "It's not whether you win or lose, it's how you place the blame!" In our age of euphemism, the drug addict has become "chemically dependent." The delinquent is suffering from "a behavioral disorder caused by preexisting conditions." And ever-greater numbers of murderers plead insanity, convincing ever-greater numbers of juries. But one way or another, our actions cause consequences. "To every action," as Sir Isaac Newton observed, "there is always opposed an equal reaction." Good begets good and evil leads to more evil. This is one of the universe's eternal, fundamental truths: the law of cause and effect.

It means that every cause (action) will create an effect (reaction) approximately equal in intensity. Making good use of our minds, skills, and talents will bring positive rewards in our outer lives. Assuming the personal responsibility to make the best use of our talents and time will result in an enormous gain in happiness, success, and wealth. This is true of everyone.

The truly successful leaders, those who have built financial empires or accomplished great deeds for society, are those who have taken personal responsibility to heart and to soul. By being true to themselves and others, they achieve success, wealth, and inner happiness. In the end, we ourselves—far more than any outsider—are the people with the greatest ability to steal our own time, talents, and accomplishments.

Responsibility psychology is a field of study pioneered by Abraham Maslow and carried on by Carl Rogers, William Glasser, Viktor Frankl, David McClelland, Albert Bandura, Nathaniel Branden, and other prominent scientists. It holds that irresponsibility and the lack of values leads to abnormal behavior, neurosis, and mental deterioration. Treatment for victims of those afflictions focuses on showing them that they are responsible for their present actions and future behavior, although they need not be hung up on the past. This school of psychology is optimistic about human growth and potential. Its practitioners have found that when neurotics are helped to assume personal responsibility, the prognosis for recovery is good. Case after case has demonstrated that responsible self-control leads to sound mental health.

I'm fond of a story from the Old Testament book of Leviticus about a sacred ceremony called "The Escaped Goat." This story led to a term—*scapegoat*—we use today when we find someone to blame for our problems. When the people's troubles became overwhelming in those early days, a healthy male goat was led into the temple. The tribe's highest priest placed his hand on the animal's head and solemnly recited the long list of the people's woes. Then the goat was released—and it ran off, supposedly taking the human troubles and evil spirits with him. That was over four thousand years ago, but the concept of the scapegoat remains in full force today. Blaming someone else or something else for our problems is nearly as old as civilization—and stays consistently young. When Adam ate of the apple, he quickly pointed at Eve. "The woman you've put here with me made me do it," he said.

We, in the industrialized nations, live at a time of incredible abundance. We enjoy material riches and a civic and legal inheritance that people of other countries continue to die for, and we take those riches for granted. But like so many successful societies in history, we may be squandering our resources and past rewards faster than we're replenishing our investment for future harvesting. That has become obvious to almost everyone but ourselves. It's dangerous enough to simply rest on one's laurels. Worse than that, we may actually be engaged in pawning them.

Perhaps the major explanation for success among Asian and other developing nations is their willingness to work very hard for the sake of future rewards. Their tolerance for sacrifice gives them an enormous social and financial force. Asian workers save an estimated 20 percent of their spendable income, more than triple the percentage of American savings. In Asia, this is called discretionary income, signifying recognition of a choice to spend or to save it. In America, we call it disposable income. And we do hasten to dispose of it—in pursuits, moreover, that tend to relieve tension instead of achieving a goal.

We protest for individual liberty and social order in the same breath. We strive for material wealth, hoping that spiritual riches will come with it as a bonus. We plead for more protection from crime but demand less interference in our social habits. We want to cut taxes and build our own empires—at the same time, we want our government to provide more financial security. But we can't have it both ways. If we want results, we must pay the price. So far we've been dealing with the symptoms. The secret is in changing the cause.

The various separate causes of most of our social problems are undermined by one major cause. Throughout my forty years of traveling—of interviewing students, teachers, parents, business and civic leaders, astronauts, former POWs, Olympic champions, factory workers, clergy, and health professionals— one message has come through loud and clear. It is that reading, writing, and arithmetic are critically important but of little use without responsibility, the fourth and missing "R." I believe the greatest single cause of problems among industrialized nations is the irresponsible obsession with immediate sensual gratification.

We want love without commitment. We want benefit packages without productivity requirements. Increasingly, we want children who demand little more from us in the way of leadership than our pets do. This is selfishness and narcissism in action. If it feels good now, just do it, baby. To achieve emotional security, each of us must develop two critical abilities: the ability to live with change and uncertainty, and the ability to delay immediate gratification for the sake of long-range goals.

Here are some action steps to help you gain more personal responsibility in your business and personal life:

Carry this affirmative motto with you: My rewards in life will reflect my service and contribution.

Set your own standards rather than comparing yourself to others. Successful people know they must compete with themselves, not with others. They run their own races.

I have learned to take more personal responsibility for my choices in life by practicing the simple urgings in The Serenity Prayer by Rheinhold Neibuhr: "God, please grant me the serenity to accept the things I cannot change, the courage to change the things I can, and the wisdom to know the difference." This means that I *accept the unchangeable*, which is everything that has already happened. That is history and cannot be changed. So I harbor my pleasant memories and gain perspective from the problems in my past. My only control is to *change the changeable*, which is my response to what has happened and my decisions in this present moment in time. Becoming a change master is to accept with serenity what has happened and courageously taking positive action in the here and now.

There was a very cautious man, who never laughed and never cried.

He never won, he never lost, he played it safe and never tried.

He went to work, earned his bread, he watched TV, and went to bed;

He felt secure, he felt no pain, he took no risk, he made no gain.

And when one day he passed away, his insurance was denied;

For since he never really lived, they claimed he never died!

Losers let it happen. Winners make it happen. Stop stewing and take control by doing.

Question: What do you think about the statement: "Your rewards in life will reflect the quality and amount of service you render"? Or more simply, do you believe "what goes around, comes around"?

Actions: Accept the unchangeable—that which has already happened. Change the changeable, your positive response and action to what is happening. Remove yourself from the unacceptable. Don't engage in group griping or pity parties. Hang out with doers instead of doomsayers.

There are two primary choices
in life: to accept conditions
as they exist or accept the
responsibility for changing them.

Real motivation is that drive
from within: You know where
you are going because you have
a compelling image inside, not
a travel poster on the wall.

Chapter 5

Reward Motivation—
Desire (Not Fear) Wins

REWARDS VERSUS PENALTIES

Desire motivation is the inner drive that keeps you moving forward in pursuit of your goals. Winners in every field in the game of life are driven by desire. There never has been a consistent winner in any profession who didn't have that burning desire to win internalized. Although philosophers and great thinkers have preached it as a basic axiom in life for centuries, this concept was first presented in an audio program by Earl Nightingale in his platinum recording of "The Strangest Secret." The strangest secret is that we become what we think about most of the time. In other words, we, our team, and our children are motivated every day and moved by our current dominant thoughts. We are moved in the direction of what we dwell on. Everyone in life is self-motivated—a little or a lot—positively or negatively. Even a decision to do nothing is a decision based on motivation.

Motivation is a very emotional state and the great physical and mental motivators in life such as survival, hunger, and thirst, as well as love and revenge, are all charged with emotion. And the two key emotions which dominate all human motivation, with opposite but nearly equally effective results, are fear and desire. Fear, of course, is the most powerful, negative motivator of all. Fear is the great inhibitor that restricts, tightens, and panics and is the red light that tells us that we can't do things because of the obstacles and risks.

Fear is the great compeller that forces us to do things that we feel we have to do because of the consequences. I remember feeling those symptoms when I was twelve years old, and my friends dared me to run through a farmer's pasture that had the biggest, ugliest, meanest bull I'd ever seen corralled there. Above the fence that we were supposed to crawl through before sprinting safely to the other side was a cryptic sign the farmer had posted for trespassers: "Don't attempt to cross this field unless you can do it in 9.9 seconds. The bull can do it in 10 flat!" That sign motivated several involuntary muscle spasms in me, and I had to change into a fresh pair of jeans when I got home. I'd much rather run toward something I want, like a ripe watermelon in that farmer's field, than have to run away from something I fear, like that bull's horns.

Desire, conversely, is like a strong, positive magnet. It attracts, reaches, opens, directs, and encourages us toward our goals. Fear and desire are poles apart, and they lead to alternate destinies in life. Fear usually looks to the past, at missed opportunities and problems, while desire looks toward the future. Fear vividly replays haunting experiences of failure, pain, disappointment, or unpleasantness and is a dogged reminder that the same experiences are likely to repeat themselves.

But desire, on the other hand, triggers memories of pleasure and success. It excites the need to replay these positive memories and create new, winning experiences. The consuming, prison words of the fearful person are likely to be "I have to." And "I can't." "I see risk." And "I wish." Desire says, "I want to. I can." "I see opportunity." And "I will." Desire is that emotional state between where you are and where you want to be. So, desire is a magnetic tension like a bow pulled taut to fire the arrow to the bull's-eye. Is tension good or bad? Yes, it is good or bad depending on whether it is initiated by fear or desire. Negative tension induced by fear creates distress, anxiety, and hostility. Carried to extremes it can cause psychosis and serious illness. But positive tension produced by desire is like an Olympic athlete coming out of the starting blocks or like that bow pulled taut to propel the arrow to the bulls'-eye. Fear causes compulsion distress.

Desire causes propulsion power. Fear causes inhibition distress. Desire causes ignition power. In a totally tension-free state, you're either in a deep, relaxed state of meditation, asleep, or dead. What a person really needs in life is not a tension-free state but the striving and struggling for a goal that is worthy of him or her. Winners have learned how to concentrate on the desired results, rather than possible problems. And winners dwell on the rewards of success, instead of the penalties of failure.

To conquer your fear of rejection, you need to handle the word "no" in a constructive way. When people turn you down after a presentation, you have to interpret the "no" as "no this is not right for me now." We also can interpret "no" as meaning,

"I need to know more about this opportunity or the products before I can say yes." I look at the service I offer to others as a gift that almost everyone desires. It's like a nutritious dessert. What if waiters or waitresses in a restaurant said to customers at their tables: "Would you like our special strawberry parfait for dessert? It's the best in the world!"

And they were told "no" by their patrons, three out of five times. Would they go to their manager, throw up their hands and quit, lamenting, "They don't like me or my strawberry parfait?" Of course they wouldn't. They'd go on about their business, thinking the patrons had missed out on something delicious. That's why you should treat the products or services you offer as a gift, much more beneficial than a fruit dessert. But what is being rejected is the presentation, not the presenter. When I can separate my self-esteem from offering the products or business opportunity, I can live with rejection and look for ways to get a positive response more often.

When you are experiencing rejection, that's the time to net-work with mentors and role models. It's also the time to listen to upbeat music and read books like this, to attend meetings and conference calls, and to hang around with optimists and winners. All you really need to move up to the next level is have faith in yourself and to risk that your ideas may not be accepted by others today but may be tomorrow or next month. Did you know eighty percent of all new sales are made after the fifth call to the same prospect. Forty-eight percent of all salespersons make one call, then cross off the prospect. Twenty-five percent quit after the second call. Twelve percent of all sales representatives call three times, then quit. Ten percent keep calling and networking until they succeed.

The sales reps in what I call the top ten percent club are among the highest paid professionals, in all industries, in the country. The ten percent who persist get the real payoff.

To win you must continuously motivate yourself toward your goals. And you must be willing to do this yourself. Be willing to say to yourself, "I'm on the right road. I'm doing OK. I'm succeeding."

We too frequently become adept at identifying our flaws and failures. Become equally adept at recognizing your achievements. What are you doing now that you weren't doing one month ago—six months ago—a year ago? What habits have changed? Chart your progress.

Doing well once or twice is relatively easy. Real winning is consistently moving ahead. Winning is tough, in part, because it is so easy to revert back to old habits and former lifestyles. Over the long run, you need to give yourself regular feedback and monitor your performance. Reinforce yourself positively to stay on track. Don't wait for an award ceremony, promotion, friend, or mentor to show appreciation for your work. Do it yourself! Do it now. Take pride in your own efforts on a daily basis.

Set up a dynamic daily routine. Getting into a positive routine or groove, instead of a negative rut, will help you become more effective. Why is the subway the most energy efficient means of transportation? Because it runs on a track. Think of the order in your day, instead of the routine. Don't worry about sameness, neatness, or everything exactly in its place. Order is being able to do what you really choose and not taking on more than you can manage. Order frees you up. Get into the swing of a healthy, daily routine and discover how much more control you'll gain in your life.

Question: Are you more motivated by the rewards of success or the penalties of failure?

Action: Beginning today, consciously get rid of compulsion/inhibition motivation: "I have to, I can't, I'll try." Replace with propulsion/volition motivation: "I want to, I can, I will."

MOTIVATION FROM INSIDE TO OUTSIDE

Psychologists make a basic distinction between intrinsic and extrinsic motivation. Having intrinsic motivation means doing something for its own sake, like playing a game just for the joy of playing. On the other hand, extrinsic motivation pulls you by the power of some external benefit or tangible reward you'll attain by taking action, like in the case of a professional athlete who plays primarily for money rather than for the fun or challenge of the sport. It also, for example, influences business and sales executives who are driven fundamentally by the income they receive rather than by the love of the service they provide. Of course, extrinsic motivation can be very powerful. Many people go to a job they neither enjoy nor care about just to receive a paycheck. You can bet these people would not go to their job every day if they knew no one was going to pay them for their work. Some of these people actively hate their jobs, but the extrinsic motivation is strong enough to keep them going faithfully every day.

Suppose you choose a particular career because of the money. What happens when there's more money in doing something else? Since there is no inner drive to stay on any particular path, the journey will be arduous, and motivation will tend to weaken whenever the external reward seems remote or out of sight. Some people spend their entire lives wandering from one field to another, always looking for an easier way to find that pot of gold, never achieving a significant goal worthy of their inner potential.

But how powerful is extrinsic motivation in a larger sense? How does the power of extrinsic compare to intrinsic motivation when the topic is doing one's best, peak performance, or human greatness? For instance, you may recall from history that the exquisitely beautiful armless statue of Venus de Milo was carved by an unknown sculptor.

When a farmer dug up the soon-to-be world-famous work of art while plowing his field, a renowned museum official sadly reflected what a great pity it was that the sculptor would never be recognized by thousands of admirers, nor would he ever know how valuable the statue became hundreds of years later. The farmer retorted that it must have been a labor of love for someone to be able to have envisioned such perfection and bring it forth with just a chisel and a shapeless piece of stone. "Just creating something of such quality," said the farmer, "would have been payment in full for me." You can't commission a masterpiece. Human greatness can't be extrinsically motivated. It must be compelled from within.

In studying history's and present day's entrepreneurs, although many of them created great wealth, we found that they were driven more by the passion of pursuing an inner calling than in trying to become rich. Fred Smith of Federal Express was obsessed with getting packages delivered faster; Bill Gates of Microsoft was focused on software solutions to real-life problems; Stephen Spielberg was more interested in what he saw through the lens of his movie camera than he was in a college degree; and Celine Dion just loved to sing ever since she was a young girl.

Mark Zuckerberg, the billionaire founder of Facebook, did not pursue his dream because he wanted to become one of the wealthiest individuals in the world. He and his friends simply wanted an innovative way to stay connected with college buddies in his and other university campuses. His motivation was an inner force that propelled him to take action.

Do you see what that means for you? If you want to be the best—whether it's the best manager, the best salesperson, the best parent, or the best athlete on your team—you have to light that fire within yourself. Real motivation is that drive from within. You know where you're going because you have a compelling image inside, not a travel poster on the wall.

One of the classic studies of motivation that leads to achievement was done by a team of scientists under the leadership of Dr. D.N. Jackson. They identified six types of "achievement motivation." As we review each of the six motivations, ask yourself the following questions: Is this an intrinsic or extrinsic form of motivation? How strongly motivated am I by this particular type of motivation? How well does this type of motivation help me achieve my goals?

The first type of achievement motivation is Status with the Experts—in other words, gaining recognition as a leader in your field. In my case, this could be a desire to be thought of in the same league as Napoleon Hill. In your case, it could mean being treated with deference and respect by your immediate boss or manager.

The second type of achievement motivation is Acquisitiveness, which is the desire to acquire something tangible, such as a fixed sum of money, a new Mercedes, or a cabin cruiser. Many people live for the things they love, and they also hate to lose those things.

I once heard about a young man in Phoenix who came home from work exhausted and ready to wind down. If someone had told him he would be spending the night digging up his yard, he would have laughed and said, "There's no way I'm going to do anything but relax." But that was before his new bride told him she had accidentally flushed her $1,800 diamond engagement ring down the drain!

Immediately, his priorities changed. Possibly influenced by the $1,000 he still owed on the ring and the fact that it wasn't insured, he became motivated to acquire the ring—whatever it took. While he spent the night digging up and taking apart the plumbing in search of the ring, his wife spent the night with a relative to escape his foul mood. After searching all night, the young husband was convinced the ring had departed from their property, so he called the water department, and out came Phoenix's "lost diamond crew" to pick up the hunt. They installed a trap at a downstream manhole, then sent a high-pressure stream of water down the sewer pipe to flush it. One of the crew members crawled down into the manhole and fished the diamond ring out of the sewage.

Now that illustrates motivation to acquire! One small possession completely dominated this young man's being for twenty-four hours, without distraction. How strong a force is motivation to acquire in your life?

The third type of achievement motivation is Achievement via Independence, which is the desire to achieve on your own skill and merit. This could involve going through the demanding academic training to become a neurosurgeon, scientist, attorney, or any other profession where you are sought after for your ability.

The fourth type of achievement motivation is Status with Peers. This is different from Status with the Experts because, to put it bluntly, your peers may not be the experts. Many of us are motivated by how we are regarded by our friends or our fellow employees at work.

The fifth type of achievement motivation is Competitiveness, something we all know about. NBC founder David Sarnoff said, "Competition brings out the best in products and the worst in people." How important is winning to you?

The sixth and final type of achievement motivation is Concern for Excellence. Vince Lombardi, the legendary coach of the

Green Bay Packers during their pro football dynasty, believed that "the quality of a person's life is in direct proportion to their commitment to excellence, regardless of their chosen field of endeavor." Concern for excellence means that you are motivated every day to be the best you can possibly be in whatever you do.

Of the six motivation types we've covered, only two—Achievement via Independence and Concern with Excellence—are true intrinsic motivations. Not coincidentally, scientists also have found that these two motivations are the most effective in leading to significant achievement. Leaders and managers should take special note of this. You need to be careful in your use of extrinsic motivators in trying to inspire your employees over the long run. Remember, enduring motivation must ultimately come from within the individual. That is why the words *empower* and *envision* are so vital to team performance and quality. It must be their power and vision that compels them, not that of the leader.

The success of our efforts depends not so much on the efforts themselves, but rather on our motive for doing them. The greatest companies and the greatest men and women in all walks of life have achieved their greatness out of a desire to express something within themselves that had to be expressed, a desire to solve a problem using their skills as best they could.

This is not to say that many of these individuals did not earn a great deal of money and prestige for what they produced. Many did. But the key to their successes is to be found in the fact that they were motivated more by providing excellence in a product or service to fill a need than by any thought of profit. William Shakespeare, Thomas Edison, and Estee Lauder all became wealthy. Separated as they were in time and type of talent, they all were motivated by the same thing: to produce the very best, to express the very best that was in them.

The problem is money alone does not stimulate intrinsic motivation and therefore is a means, not an end. Money is like fuel for your car. It is not the destination. It is not the journey. It is only part of the transportation system. Make your "why" grab you by your very soul. You'll never be disappointed for very long. And you'll stay committed regardless of market conditions or setbacks. Dr. Martin Luther King, Jr. spoke about this as eloquently as anyone ever has when he said, "If an individual is called to be a street-sweeper, he or she should sweep streets even as Michelangelo painted, or Beethoven composed music, or Shakespeare wrote poetry. He should sweep streets so well that all the hosts of Heaven and Earth will pause and say, here lived a great street-sweeper who did his job well."

Question: Are you more motivated by material rewards, money, and status or by internal values concerning excellence and self-actualization?

Action: Since intrinsic motivation is the most enduring, really explore the internal drives among your team, your loved ones, and yourself. Start today. You may be surprised.

FOCUS ON DESIRED RESULTS

An excellent illustration of this is a true story concerning one of the most exciting World Series baseball games of the 1950s between the New York Yankees and the Milwaukee Braves. Warren Spahn, the great Milwaukee Hall-of-Famer, was on the mound for the Braves. Elston Howard, the power-hitting catcher for the Yankees, was batting at the plate. It was the classic confrontation: late innings, pitchers' duel, man on base, the deciding game of the series. The tension was paramount. The Milwaukee manager trotted out to the mound for a quick motivation conference with Warren Spahn. "Don't give Howard a high, outside pitch; he'll knock it out of the park!" were the final words as the manager finished the powwow. Warren Spahn tried not to throw the ball high and outside. He tried to relax and aim low at the inside corner. Too late! Like a neon light, the motivating image "high outside" was the dominant signal. It was a home-run pitch. Because of that one dominant thought, Milwaukee almost lost the World Series. Eddie Matthews came in with a home run to save the game for the Braves. But Warren Spahn throughout the rest of his life said, "Why would anyone ever try to motivate anyone by the reverse of what they want."

You always are motivated in the direction of your current dominant thoughts. You can't concentrate on the reverse of an idea. That's why winners dwell on the desired result and the rewards of success.

Once the brain has locked on to an idea, escaping it is almost impossible. I once played in a foursome with Lee Trevino in a celebrity pro-am golf tournament. Just before our group teed off, Lee did a little psych job on us. "Do you fellows breathe in or out during your backswing?" he inquired with seeming innocence. Preparing to tee off, I tried to put the devilishly disruptive question out of my mind—but ended thinking about it, or trying not to think about it, so insistently that I sliced my ball into the gallery of three thousand Lee Trevino groupies. Only his money golfer's wink betrayed his ploy. We never found my ball. Although contingency planning is vital and safety measures must always be in place, the lesson is not to focus on possible setbacks—not to dwell on them—even as you acknowledge the possibility that some are inevitable. If you do think too much about them, they'll overwhelm you. Keep your eyes on the ball and your mind on the goal of where you want it to land.

The FBI trains its agents to spot counterfeit bills by using real ones. The agents study, study, study—but only genuine money. They steep themselves in the characteristics of authentic one, five, ten, twenty, fifty, and hundred-dollar bills until their appraisal of them becomes virtually instinctive—at which point they also instantly recognize counterfeit bills when they encounter them. With minds uncluttered with counterfeiters' common mistakes—what might be wrong, what's usually omitted—they know what they're looking for. To specialists in the real thing, imitations seem glaringly obvious. And if you allow yourself to think about all that could go wrong or the penalties of failure, you're far more likely to hobble your performance with those penalties. Constantly tell yourself what to do, instead of what not to do.

To keep people feeling like winners in today's turbulent environment is a significant leadership challenge. Hectic schedules, changing goals, and constantly shifting priorities often times make it hard for people to see the significance of their work. An essential leadership skill is always keeping the big picture, the ultimate goal, in front of the people you're working with. People also need to be reminded of the benefits that come from their work. During World War II, parachutes were being constructed by the thousands. From the workers' point of view, the job was tedious and repetitive. It involved crouching over a sewing machine eight to ten hours a day, stitching endless lengths of colorless fabric. The result was a seamless heap of cloth. But every morning the workers were reminded that each stitch was part of a life-saving operation. As they sewed, they were asked to think that this might be the parachute worn by their husband, brother, or son. Although the work was hard and the hours long, the women and men on the assembly line understood their contribution to the larger picture. The same should be true for any work. As a leader, make sure people know how what they do benefits the health and well-being of others—not just generally, but specifically. These are the visions that drive us through tedious details to the top.

Read and listen to the news and reports of professional growth, but resist the temptation to pollute your mind with the sordid details of others' tragedies. Getting hooked on tabloid exposés will make you jaded and cynical. Select more friends and associates who are optimists and highly motivated leaders. Mutual attraction should be less in the sharing of problems than in sharing solutions and goals. Learn to stay relaxed and friendly no matter how much pressure you're under. Be constructively helpful instead of unhelpfully critical. When dealing with your associates and subordinates, don't criticize failures in front of others. Correct mistakes only in private, and allow more latitude by looking at them, whenever possible, as conceivable innovations. Open criticism of others' mistakes will make them failure avoiders who will stop innovating and experimenting. Above all, put your desires and goals in positive terms. Live to greet success, not to avoid failure.

Here are a few action reminders to develop this winning action quality of reward motivation to keep the inner fires of desire burning intensely.

1. Remember: "We become what we think about." Focus all your attention and energy on the achievement of the objectives you are involved in right now.

2. Forget about the consequences of failure. Failure is only a temporary change of direction to set you straight for your next success. The person interested in success has to learn to view failure as a healthy, inevitable part of the process of getting to the top. So make a pact with yourself. We suggest you write an agreement with yourself. Promise that you won't allow a failure to be more than a learning experience that allows you to move more quickly to the place you want to be.

3. Forget perfection. Only the saints are perfect—and, "Sainthood is acceptable only in saints."

Accept the flaws and the failures in yourself and consider them challenges and learning experiences. They are seeds of growth.

Whatever you do, never allow your goals and their benefits to you to get lost in the back of your subconscious. Bring them out in the sunlight and shine them every day—and there's no way you can fail. A fear is a goal in reverse. Dwell on the problem and it grows. Dwell on finding a solution and the mind moves toward that dominant thought. Losers dwell on the penalties of failure. Winners dwell on the rewards of success. Your expectation is what drives your motivation.

To laugh is to risk appearing the fool. To weep is to risk appearing sentimental. To reach out for another is to risk involvement. To expose your feelings is to risk revealing your true self. To place your ideas and dreams before a crowd is to risk rejection. To love is to risk not being loved in return. To live is to risk dying. To hope is to risk despair. To try is to risk failure. But risks must be taken because the greatest hazard in life is to risk nothing at all. People who will risk nothing—do nothing, have nothing, and become nothing. They may avoid suffering and sorrow, but they cannot learn, feel, change, grow, love, or live. Chained by their certitudes, they are slaves. They have forfeited their freedom. Only a person who risks is truly free. And one last idea you can live and believe is the more that you give, the more you'll receive.

Question: Are you a failure-avoider? In other words, is the penalty of failure preventing you from taking risks that can result in creativity, innovation, and more success?

Action: Today view failure as fertilizer, a temporary inconvenience, a learning experience, and a necessary target correction. Those who risk nothing avoid failure and any opportunity for success. Dare to take a risk today.

Failure should be our teacher, not our undertaker. Failure is delay, not defeat. It is a temporary detour, not a dead end.

Expect the best, plan for the worst, and prepare to be surprised.

Chapter 6

The Mind/Body Effect:
Optimism Is Contagious

BELIEF IS THE KEY

When we talk about faith—and belief—we have to turn to the Scriptures. "Go your way, and as you have believed, so be it done unto you." That simple statement cuts both ways, like a two-edged sword or a lock and key. Belief is the key that can unlock the right door for everyone, the means for getting rid of the lock that imprisons people, keeping them from ever knowing success. It is a power everyone has but few consciously use. No individual possesses more of it than any other. Therefore, the question isn't whether we have faith, it's whether we use it correctly.

Belief as a positive force is the promise of realizing things hoped for and unseen. As a negative force, it is the premonition of our deepest fears and unseen darkness. Many people lead lives of quiet desperation, having many days and nights spent in a state of anxiety. There's no such thing as an absence of faith; it's always one kind or another—optimism, or cynicism and despair.

Much has been written for centuries about the self-fulfilling prophecy. A self-fulfilling prophecy is a statement that is neither true nor false but that may become true if believed. We have lectured and written much about the fact that the mind can't distinguish between things real and things vividly imagined—which is why faith and belief are so important. For example, when our fears and worries turn into anxiety, we suffer distress. Distress activates our endocrine system, changing the production of hormones and antibodies. Our immune system becomes less active; our resistance levels are lowered; we become more vulnerable to bacteria, viruses, and other ever-present hazards.

One of the leading authorities in the world on the self-expectancy relationship between mind and body is Dr. Herbert Benson, author of the best-selling book *The Relaxation Response* and *The Mind/Body Effect*, which documents the emotional relationship to many diseases.

In *The Mind/Body Effect*, Benson brilliantly explains the close interrelation between your mind and body in which thought processes lead both to disease and to good health. The concept of "voodoo death" is the extreme example of the potential negative effects of the mind on the body. In the Western world, many equivalents to "voodoo death" have been discovered in case histories. "You will die," the fortune teller predicted, "when you are forty-three." That prediction was made thirty-eight years before, when the fortune teller's client was five years old. The little girl grew up with the awesome prediction on her mind and died one week after her forty-third birthday, said a report in the *British Medical Journal*. "We wonder if the severe emotional tensions of this patient superimposed on the physiological stress of surgery had any bearing upon her death," the doctor said. They suggested she many have been frightened to death and said the case was that of an apparently healthy woman, a mother of five, who underwent a relatively minor operation. Two days later she was dead. The doctor said that the night before the woman confessed to her sister (who knew of the fortune telling incident) that she did not expect to awaken from the anesthesia. On the morning of the operation, the woman told a nurse she was certain she was going to die, but her fears were unknown to the doctors. An hour after the operation she collapsed and lost consciousness. A postmortem examination revealed extensive internal bleeding for which there was no reasonable explanation. A spokesman for the British Medical Association said, "There is no medical explanation to account for this. It seems rather like the case of the natives who die at the date and on the time the witch doctor predicts."

There is evidence that some forms of asthma are psychosomatic—more related to a smothering relationship with a doting parent ("smother love") than to outside allergens. In some cases, pictures of goldenrod were enough to bring on attacks of hay fever. In many cases, what we expect to happen, what we believe will happen, makes it happen. The powerful loneliness and hurt associated with what we call a broken heart can indeed lead to heart problems. There is also an apparent link between bottled-up emotions and the growth of some cancerous tumors. Some splitting headaches might be precipitated by being pulled in opposite directions. A rigid personality and suppressed rage have been identified as factors in some cases of arthritis.

No doubt you're familiar with the placebo effect. (Placebo literally means "I shall please.") Placebos are inert substances given to some volunteers in a given study while other volunteers are treated with experimental drugs—whose effect is tested by measuring the difference in response to the powerless placebo and to the drug. Some of a group of volunteers who had just had their wisdom teeth extracted were given morphine to alleviate their pain; the others swallowed a placebo they believed to be morphine. Many of the placebo recipients said they experienced dramatic relief from their pain. However, when a drug that blocks the effects of the endorphin was given them, the pain returned almost immediately. The test confirmed something very important: When a patient believes he or she has been given a pain reliever, the brain releases chemicals to substantiate that belief. In some cases, the brain produces chemicals previously inhibited or impaired in individuals with certain diseases. Parkinson's disease patients were given a placebo they were told was an anti-Parkinson's drug. As a result, their ability to move increased. Brain scans revealed that their brains became activated in the areas that control movement and that dopamine was being produced naturally by the brain's own pharmacy.

I share with many audiences a true story about a man named Nick. Nick, a strong, healthy railroad yardman, got along well with his fellow workers and was consistently reliable on the job. However, he was a deep pessimist who invariably feared the worst. One summer day, the train crews were told they could quit an hour early in honor of the foreman's birthday. When the other workmen left the site, Nick, the notorious worrier, was accidentally locked in an isolated refrigerated boxcar that was in the yard for repairs. He panicked. He shouted and banged until his voice went hoarse and his fists were bloody. The noises, if anyone heard them, were assumed to be coming from a nearby playground or from other trains backing in and out of the yard. Nick reckoned the temperature in the car was zero degrees. "If I can't get out," he thought, "I'll freeze to death."

He found a cardboard box. Shivering uncontrollably, he scrawled a message to his wife and family. "So cold, body's getting numb. If I could just go to sleep. These may be my last words." The next morning, the crew slid open the boxcar's heavy doors and found Nick's body. An autopsy revealed that every physical sign indicated he had frozen to death. But the car's refrigeration unit was inoperative. The temperature inside was about 61 degrees and there was plenty of fresh air. Nick's fear had become a self-fulfilling prophecy. So be careful what you believe and pretend—it may come to pass.

Our brains are so amazing that they can be trained to create the opposite effect of the negative, voodoo-like true story of Nick. It was a Saturday in November and Arnold Lemerand was taking a stroll. He heard some children screaming and hurried over to where they had been playing near a construction site. A massive cast-iron pipe had become dislodged and had rolled down on top of the children, pinning five-year-old Philip Toth against the earth. The boy's head was being forced into the dirt directly under the huge pipe and certain suffocation appeared to be imminent.

Arnold Lemerand looked around but there was no one to help him in the attempted rescue. He did the only thing he could. He reached down and lifted the 1,800-pound cast-iron pipe off Philip's head. After the incident, he tried again to lift the pipe and could not even budge it. His grown sons tried to move it, but they failed as well. In an interview later with the Associated Press, Mr. Lemerand, who was 56 at the time, said that he had suffered a major heart attack six years before. "I try to avoid heavy lifting," he smiled, with the young boy's arms around his neck. I called him to verify the story, and it was true.

We read about such miraculous power surges every so often, don't we? We hear of grandmothers lifting cars and firemen making impossible rescues in burning buildings, exhibiting superhuman strength. Those kinds of stories used to sound rather tall to me, since I've always been a man to check the source and document the advice that people give me as to its validity. I began to learn about how the mind can affect the body and how our thoughts can give us a natural high or make us ill. I was in Sarasota, Florida, serving as president of the International Society for Advanced Education, a nonprofit foundation formed by Dr. Jonas Salk and other leading health scientists to study preventive medicine and a holistic approach to wellness. The society was sponsoring continuing medical education seminars in co-operation with the University of Pittsburgh, the University of Nebraska, Johns Hopkins University, Harvard University, and other medical schools. At some of the seminars many years ago, presenters described research documenting the existence of substances in our brains similar to morphine and heroin. Over thirty years ago, they located receptor areas in the brain, which act as "locks" that only these unknown substances would fit, like "keys." It was discovered that our brains contained these "keys" in the form of natural hormones. Several have been identified, including enkephalin, endorphin, beta-endorphin, and dynorphin. All of these hormones serve as natural pain relievers many times more powerful than morphine. Beta-endorphin is one hundred and ninety times more potent than morphine.

Scientists already knew that hormones play an important role in regulating certain functions of our biological processes. Adrenalin is the hormone that enables us to "fight or flee," in the face of danger or in response to a call for peak physical performance. Insulin regulates the sugar levels in our blood. Now these later discoveries have proven that morphine-like hormones are being manufactured in our own bodies to block pain and give us a "natural high." In one test, using endorphin supplied by The Salk Institute, Japanese researchers injected minute amounts of the hormone into fourteen men and women suffering intense pain from cancer. From a single injection, they all felt relief from their pain for one to three days. In another experiment, fourteen expectant mothers were given endorphin during labor. All reported immediate and lasting pain relief and delivered normal babies.

You've heard of the "vicious cycle" in which one problem gives way to another problem, leading back to the first problem. Negative thinking deprives the body of endorphins, leading to depression, leading back to more negative thinking. Now, let's reverse the process. There is growing scientific evidence that positive mental attitudes and beliefs actually create a natural "high" to help the individual withstand pain, overcome depression, turn stress into energy, and gather strength to persevere. Physical exercise also aids in this process. In one related study, actors were wired to electrodes and connected to blood catheters. They were then asked to perform various scenes. When they portrayed characters who were angry or depressed or without hope, endorphin levels dropped. But when the scene called for emoting joy, confidence, and love, endorphins increased dramatically.

If our thoughts can cause the brain to release adrenalin from the adrenal glands to help a 56-year-old heart patient lift an 1,800-pound pipe off a boy's head, and if our thoughts can produce natural endorphins (even when we are acting out roles) that are fifty to one hundred and ninety times as powerful as morphine, is it not possible for us to use this power of optimism in our everyday lives, with the only side effect being happiness? When people ask me why I'm so optimistic and high on life, I tell them, "I'm on endorphins." They say, "It figures. We knew you were on something. "

Question: What do you feel about the statement, "What the mind harbors, the body manifests in some way"?

Action: Think and speak well of your health today. There is a psychosomatic relationship between your thoughts and your physiological responses.

CHALLENGES AS OPPORTUNITIES

One of the most desirable attitudes of a prospective employee, leader, or manager is an ability to see challenges as opportunities, setbacks as temporary inconveniences. This positive attitude also welcomes change as friendly and is not upset by surprises, even negative surprises. How we approach challenges and problems is a crucial aspect of our decision-making process, whether in business or in our personal lives.

In the 1920s, when Ernest Hemingway was working hard to perfect his craft, he lost a suitcase containing all his manuscripts—many stories he'd laboriously polished to jewel-like perfection—which he'd been planning to publish as a book. The devastated Hemingway couldn't conceive of redoing his work. He could think only of the months he'd devoted to his arduous writing—and for nothing, he was now convinced. But when he lamented his loss to the poet Ezra Pound, Pound called it a stroke of luck. Pound assured Hemingway that when he rewrote the stories, he would forget the weak parts; only the best material would reappear. Instead of framing the event in disappointment, Pound cast it in the light of opportunity. Hemingway did rewrite the stories—and the rest, as they say, is history: He became one of the major figures in American literature.

In companies and environments in which criticism, pessimism, cynicism, and motivation by fear prevail, a condition develops that I see all too often in business. Fear of failure leads to avoiding failure at all costs. The trouble with failure avoidance is that it's simultaneously avoidance of success, which depends on taking risks. Innovation and creativity are impossible when employees are afraid because they're penalized for failure. The first play of Charles Lamb, a celebrated British essayist and critic, was hissed off the stage. Seated in the audience, Lamb was so afraid of being identified as the author that he hissed too. Tennessee Williams's first play was booed so loudly that the producers came forward and apologized to the audience.

Early experience usually teaches that failure is to be avoided at all costs. This begins in childhood, when we encounter the first "No!" It grows like a weed when we are criticized by our parents and other family members, by our teachers, and by our peers. It leads to associating ourselves with our mistakes, to a self-image of clumsiness and awkwardness.

Fear of failure can become a built-in motivation. Leaders like to succeed and feel good about themselves; fearful people, focused on failure avoidance so as not to feel worse about themselves, refuse to try. External factors can also boost fear of failure. If, for example, half a division must be laid off, factory or office workers who have long performed well may be seized by the diminishing, damaging fear. I presented an employee-productivity program to a large division of a Fortune 500 company manufacturing integrated circuit boards in competition with the Japanese. After my talk about leadership lessons, the huge facility's general manager mounted the stage and gave his two thousand workers what he thought was a parting motivational message. "What we must have from all of you is a 17 percent increase in quality production in six months, or we're faced with closing down the plant. Have a good weekend."

His words had the predictable effect. The leaders and achievers increased their performance by about 20 percent. But many non-achievers found more secure jobs and quit within weeks— and the plant did shut down after about six months. This was more confirmation that genuine leaders focus on the benefits of success, while those chiefly motivated by fear concentrate on failure's painful consequences. Some bosses and managers argue that employees motivated by fear work as hard or even harder than those with positive motivations. They are deluding themselves. Fear motivation is as obsolete as communism because it simply doesn't work as an effective leadership tool.

Psychological research proves that people who fear failure are more likely to fail in assignments of medium difficulty—those with approximately equal chances of success or failure—than those without such fears. This is true even when the failure-avoiders are better qualified for particular assignments than their more positively motivated colleagues. Anxiety about failure doesn't merely diminish performance. It also stifles the motivation to succeed in the first place.

Learned helplessness is a belief that we're at the mercy of external forces and no longer in control of what is happening to us. Behaviorists emphasize that this feeling is indeed learned. Martin Seligman, a psychologist at the University of Pennsylvania and author of the best-selling *Learned Optimism*, has made a very detailed study of learned helplessness—and confirms it's a trait we acquire, not inherent at birth.

My friends have an English bulldog named Spike, who looks so ferocious that he scares everyone who comes to visit his owners. Actually, Spike is quite gregarious and fun loving. He wants to welcome the guests by jumping up on them, giving them a big hug and kiss, and tattooing his friendly paw and claw marks on their clothes and skin. Much to his dismay, Spike usually gets locked out of the room when visitors are present.

To make him socially acceptable, Spike gets a weekly bath. His owner fastens his thick, leather leash on his choke chain and says enthusiastically, "Let's go take our nice bath!" Spike puts on his brakes by digging all four paws into the carpet and refuses to budge one muscle of his sixty-pound, solid, Arnold Schwarzenegger-like physique. His owner has to use all her strength to literally drag him outside and across the patio to the designated post where she gives him—and much of the time herself, as well—a bath. Witnessing this struggle gives you an idea of Spike's strength and ingenuity.

Recently, Spike's family had a group of about twenty people over. Several wanted Spike to be allowed in the house so they could play with him, but most were afraid of what he might do. Spike's owner put on his leash and brought him in the house. Much to the delight of most of the guests, he jumped and ran from guest to guest, checking them out and dragging his owner with him at the end of the leash. He grabbed his ball and indicated that he wanted to play his favorite ball game: keep away. Nothing could hold Spike down—except his leash.

His owner took him over to a small antique chair weighing about five pounds, lifted one of the legs, put the loop of his leash around the leg, and walked away. Spike looked forlorn and helpless. Everyone said, "That chair won't hold him. He's going to get loose and jump on us and get revenge because we won't play ball with him!" "I know the chair won't restrain him," said the owner, "but Spike doesn't know it."

Totally put down, submissive, and disappointed—we might even say depressed—Spike sat through the duration of the party with his leather leash held down by a five-pound chair with no one sitting on it. No one told Spike to stay and that he couldn't move. He hadn't been to obedience school. He simply assumed he couldn't move because when he has his bath, that leash is fastened to a post, and he can't get away. So he doesn't even try to move the chair for fear of the same results.

Unfortunately, too many of us are like Spike. We find ourselves in a situation in which we assume we're helpless and we give up. Some past experience tells us we can't move ahead, and we give up without even trying.

Some years ago, I held a seminar for an NFL Super Bowl champion team that was trying to repeat a near-perfect season. A clinical hypnotist also on the program demonstrated how easy it is to learn helplessness. He put a burly fullback into a state of relaxation, then placed a three-ounce paperweight on the locker room floor, suggesting it weighed five hundred pounds. Then he asked the mighty fullback, who could ordinarily bench press a stocked freezer, to pick it up. "If it weighs five hundred pounds," the player replied, "I don't think I can lift it." But he tried. He strained and puffed. His face turned purple, the veins on his arms distended—but he couldn't budge the little glass cube. We all suspected this was a comedy act the two had worked up for laughs. But when the fullback's biceps were monitored with biofeedback instruments, they indicated that he was pulling up with a force that would have lifted a four-hundred-pound barbell from the floor. Why did he fail with the three-ounce paperweight? The same instruments measuring his triceps indicated that they were pushing down to keep the paperweight where he "knew" it belonged—pushing down, it was established, with more force than he was using to try to lift it.

The larger explanation was that the powerful man's mind forced him to work against himself so that he could confirm his picture of an immovable object on the floor. Thus, an idea he accepted made him his own worst enemy. How often we hypnotize ourselves or our employees or children into believing we're helpless victims of external circumstance when actually that's what we've chosen to believe. If you ever feel you're trying your hardest but getting nowhere, take a moment to ask yourself whether you really believe you can succeed. If you're not truly convinced of the possibility, make a conscious effort to clear your mind of learned helplessness. Think of the fullback who had the physical ability to toss the little paperweight through the Superdome roof when he wasn't fighting himself.

One of the best ways to overcome learned helplessness and to help employees and others become positively motivated is to break down long-term goals into smaller, nearer ones so that a high expected probability of success can be maintained. We would choke on a steak if we tried to swallow it all in one go, but bite-size pieces give us several kinds of longer-lasting delight. It's easier to keep moving toward an initial, more reachable goal and also easier to correct our course if we miss. Attaining smaller goals helps us believe we can achieve our larger ones, increasing our perception of success for even the most complex designs.

Sports and industrial psychologists have studied goal setting carefully. Working with our Olympic athletes over many years, my colleagues and I learned to emphasize that the decathlon, for example, was a series of ten sub-goals; that marathon races had a series of sub-goals, with benchmarks along their routes. Almost every gold medal winner in sports and business forms an aerial view of his or her race as a whole, then uses smaller goals as progress guides and positive motivational reinforcements. Goals must be specific and vivid in order to be visualized with real pulling power. Although the human mind, the most marvelous computer ever created, can consider nebulous general thoughts, the more specific the input, the more detailed the image for generating motivational force. We will cover focused goals in the coming weeks.

Question: Do you know examples of people who are consumed by "learned helplessness"? They are the pessimists who see a problem in every possible solution. Are you aware that Nostradamus has become a timeless soothsayer because he spent his life predicting catastrophes?

Action: When others attempt to rain on your parade, grab an invisible umbrella and stay optimistic. When you begin the day and end the day, find something positive to say to encourage "learned optimism."

INCURABLE OPTIMISM

There's a wonderful story, first told by educator Edward Pulling, about finding joy while working in the most mundane jobs. Back in the Middle Ages, a dispatcher went out to determine how laborers felt about their work. He went to a building site in France. He approached the first worker and asked: "What are you doing?" "What, are you blind?" the worker snapped back. "I'm cutting these impossible boulders with primitive tools and putting them together the way the boss tells me to. I'm sweating under the blazing sun, it's backbreaking work, and it's boring me to death!"

The dispatcher quickly backed off and retreated to a second worker. He asked the same question: "What are you doing?" The worker replied: "I'm shaping these boulders into useable forms, which are then assembled according to the architect's plans. It's hard work and sometimes gets repetitive, but I earn five francs a week and that supports the wife and kids. It's a job. Could be worse."

Somewhat encouraged, the dispatcher went on to a third worker. "And what are you doing?" he asked. "Why can't you see!" beamed the worker, as he lifted his arm to the sky. "I'm building a beautiful cathedral!" Life is a perception through the eyes of the beholder.

What you visualize and internalize, you must realize can materialize. Research done by the Yale School of Public Health and the National Institute on Aging found that young people who had positive perceptions about aging were less likely to have a heart attack or stroke when they grew older. And another study confirmed that middle-aged and elderly people lived an average of seven years longer if they had a positive perception of aging.

How does your lifestyle—your expectations and your fore-casting—affect your own health and well-being? Optimism is an incurable condition in the person with faith. Optimists believe that most disease, distress, dysfunction, and disturbance can be remedied. Optimists also are prevention and wellness oriented.

Their thoughts and actions are focused on solutions, health, and success. They concentrate on positive outcomes and rewards, rather than the penalties of failure.

What the mind harbors, the body manifests. This is especially important when you are raising children or leading a team. Focus on the well family and dwell on health as the usual environment around your house. We have seen more psychosomatic illnesses in homes where the parents dote on and smother the children with undue concern for their health and safety than in any other type of household. We believe in safety precautions and sound medical practice. We also believe that "your worst" or "your best" concerns will likely come to pass. Through many decades in dealing with Olympic athletes, professional sports' franchises and companies, the highest performers invariably have had the most optimistic daily environments. You may not get what you want in life, but, generally speaking, you are much more likely to get what you expect.

Positive self-expectancy brings positive benefits into being. The advice to whistle while you work, therefore, is more than just fairy-tale talk from a Disney character. It's very sound medical and psychological counsel. Here are specific principles that you should put into practice every day. By diligently acting on these principles, you can do more for your physical well-being than any number of pills from a bottle—and at much lower expense.

First, learn to listen to your body. Learn to distinguish between genuine requirements and mere wants or cravings. If you're out walking on a hot day and your throat is parched, you really need a drink of water, and you should have one. But if you just happen to be passing through the kitchen and your eye falls on the cookie jar, that's something else again. The desire for food, exercise, sleep, or entertainment can all arise from authentic needs or just as substitute forms of gratification. So don't fool yourself. Eat when you're hungry, drink when you're thirsty, sleep when you're tired, and make those decisions yourself. Don't let a television commercial or an advertisement in a magazine make the decision for you.

Second, live in the present moment. Seize the day! How many times have we heard athletic coaches talk about playing one game at a time? It may be a cliché, but it's got a solid core of truth. Unless you choose to endow them with importance, events from the past have no reality, and neither do fears or premonitions of the future. Everywhere we look in nature, the trees, the flowers, and the animals are all sharply focused on being exactly what they are in the present moment. If we can just learn that lesson, if we can just let go of regret and fear, we can take a huge step toward physical and emotional health.

Third, resist the ever-present temptations of anger and vindictiveness. Everyone has a million good reasons to be angry, but healthy and successful people find equally compelling reasons to be calm and happy. The physiological effects of anger—on the heart, for example—have been well documented, but even if anger weren't dangerous, it's still simply unpleasant for everyone. No one has our respect more than a person who can cultivate personal happiness amid the twists and turns of life's journey. It's a far greater and far rarer attribute than the ability to make money, shoot a basketball, or win an election. Cultivate contentment and let go of anger, and you'll live long. More importantly, you'll live well.

Fourth, learn to take off your judicial robes. At some level, each of feels we ought to rule the world. As kings or queens of creation, we would quickly straighten out everybody's mistakes and put things into good order. We all feel this way, but the wisest and healthiest of us recognize those feelings for the childish and superficial impulses that they are. We should also notice how those judgmental feelings increase in direct proportion to the dissatisfaction and frustrations that we experience in our own lives.

Here are some action ideas for more positive self-expectancy:

Optimism and realism go together. They are the problem-solving twins. Pessimism and cynicism are the two worst companions. Your best friends should be individuals who are the "No problem, it's just a little, temporary inconvenience" type. As you help other people in need on a daily basis, also develop an inner circle of close associations in which the mutual attraction is not sharing problems or needs. The mutual attraction should be values and goals.

Resist the temptation to waste time reading or watching the sordid details of someone else's tragedies. Listen to inspirational music or instructional audios in your car. If possible, have breakfast and lunch with an optimist. Instead of sitting in front of the TV at night, spend time listening to and being involved with those you love. Engage in positive recreation and education. Select TV programs specializing in the wonders of family health and cultural enrichment. Select the movies and television you watch for their quality and story value rather than their commercial appeal.

Get high on your expectations. Instead of, "Relief is just a swallow away," think of, "Belief will help you follow the way." The people you associate with, the places you go, the things you listen to and watch, all are recorded in your thoughts. Since the mind tells the body how to act, think the highest and most uplifting thoughts you can imagine.

As we have stressed throughout this book, you become what you think about most of the time. You become that to which you are most exposed. What you watch, what you hear, what you read, and your self-explanatory style have a profound influence on your outcomes in life. You are in control of the software program that runs your body and mind. The future belongs to the optimists.

Question: Are you aware that 90 percent of what you are exposed to on a daily basis is "bad news"? Do you pass on what's wrong with the world, rather than what is being done to improve it? Think about your daily dialogue and whether you are encouraging or discouraging.

Action: Commit today to fly with the eagles. Join an online community of optimists with the same goals, not the same protests. Spend lunchtime and free time, as much as possible, with winners. Your enthusiasm will be contagious.

What the mind dwells upon,
the body acts upon.

It is not in the pursuit of happiness
that we find fulfillment, it is
in the happiness of pursuit.

Chapter 7

Your Virtual World:
Imagination Rules the Future

IMAGINATION IS GREATER
THAN KNOWLEDGE

Napoleon once said, "Imagination rules the world." Einstein believed, "Imagination is more important than knowledge, for knowledge is limited to all we now know and understand, while imagination embraces the entire world, and all there ever will be to know and understand."

The human being, with no pre-recorded computer program as a life guide, is blessed with a creative imagination. This is why healthy role models and positive support, superimposed upon strong moral values, are so important. Since we are not predestined as members of a wandering herd, victimized, and imprisoned within a fixed environment, we need dreams, images, maps, and charts to guide us. In successful individuals these maps and charts are called role models and values. In unsuccessful individuals they are more like walls and ceilings.

First through our senses, during our early development— then through language and observation—we record, build, and photograph our video, audio, and sensory software. This recorded self-concept or self-image—this mental picture of self—when nourished and cultivated, is a primary field in which happiness and success grow and flourish. But this same mental self-concept, when undernourished or neglected, becomes a spawning pond for low achievement, deviant behavior, and unhappiness.

Remember during our discussion on self-esteem, we noted that many people see themselves as inadequate. The early messages recorded on their "inner software" say: "I can't do things very well, especially new things. I don't think people like the way I look. There's no sense in really trying, because I'll probably get it wrong and won't succeed anyway." These are the surprisingly large numbers of individuals in this abundant society who have the most difficulty learning and advancing and who are problems to themselves and others. Recently, I met with a psychologist who gave an intelligence test to a 12-year-old boy. Part of the test consisted of putting pieces of a jigsaw puzzle together. He tried it, but quickly gave up in frustration, saying: "I can't do it; it's too hard!" His self-image told him that if something looks like a test and you have difficulty with it, then you give up.

We have found that the successful people are those whose "inner software" carries a message something like this: "I can do things pretty well—a variety of things. I can try new challenges and be successful. When things don't go smoothly at first, I keep trying or get more information to do it in a different way until it works out right." These are the few who can, and usually do, learn the most and who can share and give the most to others from what they have learned. They have discovered that their imaginations serve as a life-governing device—that if your self-image can't possibly see yourself doing something or achieving something, you literally cannot do it.

Self-esteem is how you feel about yourself. Self-image is how you see yourself. Self-confidence is proof of your value through your actions. Winners believe in their dreams when that's all they have to hang on to. Your mind stores as reality what you vividly, repeatedly imagine. A mantra you will hear throughout this book is: "What you visualize and internalize, you can come to realize and materialize."

By the time children reach school age they have watched over 20,000 commercials, most of which teach them to consume more, and that life's problems can be solved by a certain product in 60 seconds or less. We are growing up tethered to our video-streaming smartphones, being fed sponsor-driven content. The images emanating from platforms such as Meta, Instagram, YouTube, and TikTok have become the basis for many of our beliefs and values. By the time we leave high school or college, most of us will have spent 70 percent more time in front of a screen than in the classroom or having rewarding experiences with our parents, families, and friends. We can't really blame the commercial media for the situation, because the quality of programming is only a reflection of the character of our families in today's social scene. However, with bottom-line profit driving creative programming, it's no wonder that life imitates fashion and fashion is created by those who profit by selling it. Let's remember, if a sixty-second commercial, by repeated viewing, can sell us a product, then isn't it possible for a sixty-minute fantasy reality show, by repeated viewing, to sell us a lifestyle?

Studies conducted by a Stanford University research team have revealed that "what we watch" has a major effect on our imaginations, our learning patterns, and our behaviors. First, we are exposed to new behaviors and characters. Next, we learn or acquire these new behaviors. The last and most crucial step is that we adopt these behaviors as our own. One of the most critical aspects of human development that we need to understand is the influence of "repeated viewing" and "repeated verbalizing" in shaping our future. The information goes in, "harmlessly, almost unnoticed," on a daily basis, but we don't react to it until later, when we aren't able to realize the basis for our reactions. In other words our values are being formed without any conscious awareness on our part of what is happening!

Modeling is a potent learning tool that goes far beyond simple imitation. Imitation or simulation is a conscious training process by which a person intentionally copies the behavior of someone else. Modeling takes place unconsciously, as one individual gradually assumes the characteristics of someone else, particularly someone he or she likes or admires. Creativity is seeing, in advance, an idea that can become a solution to a major problem or need and holding on to that idea until it works or until a better idea is implemented. Creativity is holding on to your dreams even when others laugh at you. Creativity comes from having mentors and coaches who are interested in your success—coaches who'll listen, unconditionally, who praise often and criticize constructively the behavior that is undesirable, while not directly criticizing the individual. Creativity is having curious leaders who are open to new ideas and to better ways of doing things and who are not so set in their ways that they prejudge everything in advance. Unimaginative and unproductive people say, "It may be possible, but it's too difficult." Creative individuals say, "It may be difficult, but it's always possible."

Question: Who do you consider as your most inspiring role model today?

Action: There is something you have wanted to do for a long time but have been putting off because it seems too selfish or unrealistic for you to pursue. Begin doing it this weekend.

MOVING FROM VIRTUAL TO REALITY

I have been imagining and fantasizing all my life, and this has been a useful escape from an early childhood environment laced with financial strife, alcohol abuse, disharmony, and divorce. I remember saying my prayers at night after my mom and dad's shouting matches about his habits and low income: "God, guide me never to drink, smoke, or get married." My father left home when I was nine, and we kids felt somehow that we were part of the cause, because of the financial burden. My mother remained negative and bitter throughout her life, and I only recall rare occasions when she offered any positive encouragement.

I had a recurring fantasy, about age 12. I was standing, in a tuxedo, in an ornate theater with beautiful chandeliers, bowing humbly before an enthusiastic audience giving me a standing ovation for what I had said or portrayed. It was so vivid and real to me. My imaginary mom and dad were in the front row, smiling, clapping along with the others, and this gave me a feeling that I had finally earned their approval. This continued until I was a young adult. I forgot about those daydreams until 40 years later, when I experienced an amazing moment of déjà vu. I actually was standing in Carnegie Hall, in New York City, in a tuxedo, receiving a standing ovation for a lecture on "The Psychology of Winning," and even though my parents were not there in person, I imagined them sitting in the front row, smiling. As I was humbly acknowledging the audience's positive response, I found myself saying silently to my missing mom and dad, "Am I OK now? Am I a good boy? A worthy son?"

Visualization, or mental simulation, is not a new concept. We all have fantasized and acted out our "life scripts"—virtual reality shows or magnificent epic movies—at some point in our lives. I have been experiencing and researching many different examples of high-performance visualization since my early years as a Navy pilot in the 1950s, later with NASA astronauts in the 1960s, and then up close and personal as chairman of psychology on the U.S. Olympic Committee's Sports Medicine Council during the 1980s.

Olympians train up to 1,200 days for a few moments of competition. Astronauts simulate until the profoundly unknown is perfectly known, the strangely unfamiliar becomes intimately familiar. I remember my own combat training as a naval aviator. My throat tightened as two enemy interceptors appeared on my radar screen. Knowing that a heat-seeking missile would be locked on to my tailpipe in seconds, I executed an aerobatic maneuver into heavy cloud cover. But I pulled too many Gs and lost control of the plane. With a bad case of vertigo, I was thrown from the cockpit by the centrifugal force of the uncontrollable spin. I fell for what seemed an eternity, about four feet, from the flight simulator onto the hangar floor. The door of the simulator had unlocked, and I'd forgotten to fasten my seatbelt. The instructors doubled up in laughter. My peers joined with some choice remarks as I lay sprawled on the control room floor. Even worse were the stares of members of Congress and other VIPs who had come to observe Naval Air Pacific warriors display their superb combat skills. Being more like Will Farrell than Tom Cruise was hard on my ego, but the fallout included an important leadership lesson.

"Just be glad this was the simulator," my instructor said, shrugging. "There are no second chances with the real thing!" What I learned that day—over fifty years ago—I later have confirmed again and again. It is that the mind can't distinguish between imagined and real experience. The mind stores as truth everything vividly rehearsed and practiced—which is why it's so vital to store winning instead of losing images. And to correct your mistakes as they are made, focusing on how to do it right next time. This is the centerpiece of our program.

My first interest in becoming involved in the Olympic movement began when I was working at The Salk Institute in La Jolla, California, about six years after leaving the Navy. I was always fascinated by the observation that, at the world-class level in any endeavor, but especially in sports, that talent is nearly equal. The winning edge to me has always been the mental edge. Mind over muscle, mind over environment, mind over circumstance. My first live Olympic experiences began in the late 1960s.

The air was thin and still on that October afternoon in 1968, and there was a hush of anticipation in the Olympic stadium. Bob Beamon had just leaped nearly thirty feet in the long jump, a record that remains unbroken as of this writing. The attention of the 84,000 spectators at the Mexico City Olympics was now centered on the high jump bar, set at 2.24 meters (approximately 7 feet 4.2 inches), a record height at the time. The athlete was a carrot-topped, freckle-faced youth by the name of Dick Fosbury, who had revolutionized the art of high jumping with the invention of a backward, headfirst dive known as the Fosbury Flop.

While the throng sat mutely, eyes glued to the bar, awaiting Fosbury's attempt, it intently studied Fosbury's pre-jump concentration. He stood about twenty yards directly in front of the bar, preparing for a straight-ahead running approach. His eyes were closed, his hands opened and closed rhythmically at his sides, and he rocked back and forth, toe to heel. This ritual continued for nearly eight minutes. The crowd began to murmur softly, becoming anxious, and the television commentator wondered aloud what was going on.

Then, with no warning, Fosbury broke into a lope that developed into a relaxed sprint. As he neared the bar he rotated his body 180 degrees on the way up, arched his back in a reverse swan dive and cleared the bar, which didn't even tremble, for a new world record.

Even more amazing than the feat of winning was Fosbury's own revelation of how he did it. In an interview after the competition we learned that Dick Fosbury, like so many other champions, was a master of visualization. As Fosbury rocked back and forth with eyes closed, he was mentally picturing every step to the bar—the push-off, the rotation, the back arch, the feet position—in advance. And when the mental rehearsal gave him a vivid picture of his success in clearing the bar, it was his signal that he was ready.

I believe I have learned more from Olympic coaches like Herb Brooks, during the "Miracle on Ice" Olympic ice hockey victory in 1980, and Olympic champions like Mary Lou Retton and Carl Lewis in 1984 than they ever learned from me. And, for the past 30 years, our institute has been able to document what we have observed in world-class athletes.

According to Michael Phelps, the most decorated Olympian of all time, his success stems from first visualizing each race before he even steps into the pool. Phelps says he's been visualizing since he was seven years old, watching what he calls his video of the perfect swim in his mind each night before going to sleep, mentally mapping out his ideal swim for the next day. Renowned Olympic gold medalist and World Cup skiing champion Lindsey Vonn says her mental practice gives her a competitive advantage on the course. She says, "I always visualize the run before I do it. By the time I get to the start gate, I've run that race 100 times already in my head, picturing how I'll take the turns." Not only does Lindsey pre-play visual images in her mind, she also simulates the path by shifting her weight back and forth as if she were on her skis, while practicing the specific breathing patterns she'll use during the race.

When asked about athletic skills versus mental skills, Michael Jordan, one of the greatest NBA basketball players of all time, said: "The mental part is the hardest part, and I think that's the part that separates the good players from the great players." In using mental imagery, Jordan said, "I visualized where I wanted to be, what kind of player I wanted to become. I knew exactly where I wanted to go, and I focused on getting there." And one of my favorite Hall of Famers-to-be, NFL legendary quarterback Peyton Manning, put it simply this way: "Some guys need to see things on a grease board; I like when you can see it in your mind!"

In every sport, visualization is in the spotlight, whether it's Michael Phelps or Carli Lloyd, member of the 2015 US women's world cup soccer championship team and the first player to ever score three goals in a World Cup final, reflecting how she takes time before each game to visualize positive scenarios between herself and the soccer ball.

Visualization is not reserved for pilots, astronauts, and athletes only. Sales executives, scientists, surgeons, Navy SEALs, dancers, musicians, actors, parents, teachers, and students do it every day. Visualization can also be used to improve health and well-being. During the past decade the techniques involved in visual imagery and mental rehearsal have grown from the oversimplified concepts of positive thinking to more scientific approaches that incorporate high-speed cinematography, digitized computer readouts and stop-action video replay, neuro-feedback techniques, and simulation technology. Certain kinds of music, colors, images, and sensory environments can evoke different brain wave and emotional responses. Virtual reality technology, which many people associate with video games, has many beneficial applications.

Visualization works because the mind reacts automatically to the information we feed it in the form of words, pictures, and emotions. And, as we have discussed, the brain's neural pathways can be reshaped and redirected. Basically there are two types of visualization—receptive and programmed. Receptive visualization is used to help answer a question or find a solution to a problem. In this type of visualization, the question is formulated or the problem posed. First the issue is analyzed logically for better understanding; then a mental picture of a blank screen is formed, and the answer or solution is allowed to appear on the screen in its own time. This technique is especially helpful in recalling information that appears to have been forgotten or lost.

Programmed visualization is used to get what we want in life. We picture what we want repeatedly, and the brain sends signals to the body that cause us to take action to bring about the desired results. Make sure you really want what you are visualizing; never picture a condition or event you don't want to occur.

Visualization can also be used to improve health and well-being. We are at the dawn of a new era in neuroscience as it applies to our health and well-being. Much has been discussed about the potential for virtual reality to transform the economy by revitalizing consumer entertainment, social media, shopping, education, and travel.

Thousands of scientists and professionals are securing new patents, and sifting through existing ones, to uncover the most innovative brain health and brain enhancement systems on the cutting edge, likely to go mainstream in the next few years. Very soon you will become aware of how virtual reality and neuroscience are making incredible strides in pain management, physical rehabilitation, and treatment of anxiety disorders, such as Post Traumatic Stress Disorder (PTSD), and phobias, such as fear of flying, fear of spiders, fear of heights, fear of needles, fear of public speaking, and claustrophobia. A number of companies are engaged in the field of real-time neuro-monitoring, developing systems to monitor brain activity and respond in real time with pre-emptive treatments.

Do you understand the potential? With a monitoring or a wearable device, it will become possible to anticipate a seizure, a possible stroke, and, at some point, a possible heart attack in advance of the event. In other words, prevention is on the near horizon. And, yes, science fiction has become science fact, in the emerging field of Brain Computer Interfaces (BCIs), which link the commands of our thoughts to many electronic devices including, but not limited to, smartphones, home appliances, biofeedback equipment, security systems, and you name it. I have always believed that thoughts would not just create material things, like ships, aircraft, spacecraft, buildings, computers, TVs, and phones. But that thoughts would be able to guide and control our material inventions for the benefit of all living things.

Einstein was right. Imagination is more important than knowledge, for knowledge is limited to all we now know and understand, while imagination embraces the entire world, and all there ever will be to know and understand. When imagination is focused on the creation of life-enhancing thoughts, dreams, emotions, and goals it becomes a brain-train breakthrough which we call Winning for Life.

Question: What do you imagine that would improve your daily life the most?

Action: Make a call, make an appointment. If necessary, find a friend or colleague to join you and set a date to begin that process.

SEEING FROM WITHIN

Over twenty years ago, the U.S. government sponsored a new television public service campaign to attract foreign tourists to America. The video promotion featured breathtaking panoramas of our national landscape. "O beautiful for spacious skies, for amber waves of grain; for purple mountains' majesty, above the fruited plain." Combined with the magnificent vistas, this song of vision has filled many eyes with tears of pride and exhilaration. The person chosen to sing it was Ray Charles, ironically, who had never seen the sky, the mountains, or the plains—which is a key point of this message. Ray Charles, Stevie Wonder, John Milton, Helen Keller, and thousands of others are or were visionaries, creating from within.

By the end of this decade, it may be possible for totally blind people to see too. They will use a neural-prosthetic device employing a television camera attached to electrodes one-third the circumference of a human hair, implanted in the visual cortex in the back of the brain. It would look something like Geordi's visor on *Star Trek: The Next Generation*. Similar auditory implants are being developed to restore hearing to the deaf, and electronic bypasses are being designed to restore motor functions for those with spinal cord injuries. The human mind has incredible potential for designing almost anything it can imagine and transmitting the blueprints anywhere in the world.

Actually, we needn't hold our breath waiting to use interactive virtual reality; its power is already available in our homes and offices—even on the golf course. One Sunday afternoon in June, I was at the Rancho Santa Fe Golf Club, near my home, celebrating one of the milestone birthdays you'd just as soon forget. It happened to be the final day of the classic Memorial tournament. I had just blown out my birthday candles—which, I'm sorry to confess, took several puffs—when I heard the crowd roar. In one of the most spectacular finishes of a major PGA tournament, Paul Azinger had chipped out of a difficult lie in a sand trap and into the cup on the final hole to beat his friend Payne Stewart for the purse. Jack Nicklaus then interviewed Azinger on national television. "You know, Paul," complimented Nicklaus, "you and I could have stood in that trap all day and thrown golf balls at the flag—and not one of them would have gone in the hole."

Azinger replied modestly that he'd actually imagined the ball going in, although he couldn't actually see the hole from where he was playing the ball. I hope I'm not one to toot my own horn, any more than Azinger. But I'll report here that I nearly dropped a forkful of cake when Azinger quoted me to Nicklaus. "Denis

Waitley's book," he said, "advised that 'You should imagine the mind to be a quart jar and always make certain it's full of positive thoughts like intentions of hitting winning shots. While many are thinking what can go wrong with the shot, winners are thinking what can go right. The winner's mind is so focused on the desired result, there can be no room for negatives.'"

"With the round I had today," Nicklaus chuckled, "maybe I should have read that book." Azinger admonished him with a smile. "Jack, the author was writing about you. I was reading about how you think and play. Waitley was only quoting you!"

Let's review some of the most important concepts we have learned so far: Self-esteem is how you feel about yourself. Self-image is how you see yourself. Self-confidence is proof of your value through your actions. Winners believe in their dreams when that's all they have to hang on to. Your mind stores as reality what you vividly, repeatedly imagine. What you visualize and internalize, you can come to realize and materialize.

Limits are physical. Limitations are psychological. Over time we all learn to raise or lower our expectations of ourselves because of our experiences. Successes give us confidence. Disappointments become solid barriers. Most people feel like thermometers. A thermometer rises or falls to meet the external environment. Most self-images are controlled by what the media and our role models bombard our senses with on a daily basis. However, we do have control of our future thoughts. We can reset our self-image like an internal thermostat from loser to winner, from average performance to peak performance, and elevate our comfort zones over time.

That's why your ongoing engagement in this and other self-development programs is so important. They become interactive training and tracking systems for everyday living. Therefore, you look at your past conditioning, and you realize you've been holding yourself back and selling yourself short. And you use new, positive inputs to layer on top of the past conditioning, and you change the future behavior and performance accordingly. The good news is, you don't have to play the part of the victim. You can rewrite your own script and become the MVP in this game of choice called life. You are your own scriptwriter, and the play is never finished. No matter what your age, position, or place in life, the truth is: Who you see is who you'll be. We can only wonder who the next Mark Zuckerberg, who founded Facebook in his college dorm room, will be. It's a matter of removing the invisible barriers of self-imposed limitations.

Question: What do you feel is holding you back most from your greatest aspirations?

Actions: Here are a few ideas to elevate your creative imagination:

Set aside 20 to 30 minutes a day relaxing and enjoying your most personal desires. See them as if you were previewing three movie previews. Picture yourself in one sequence achieving a professional triumph (imagine the award ceremony, promotion announcement, or bonus payment). Picture another sequence involving family happiness (imagine a special reunion or outing together). Picture another sequence in which you alone are relishing a personal victory (imagine a tennis or golf championship or completion of your best 500K run). Get the actual sensation of each event and how good it feels to experience each one.

When you visualize yourself doing something, make it an action scene in which there's movement. In sports psychology, this is referred to as VMBR, Visual Motor Behavior Rehearsal, and the object is to create a neurological pathway enabling your muscles to "remember" the sequence of movements that make up an action. Therefore, no still pictures please.

Visualize both the successful outcome and the steps leading up to it. Olympic athletes mentally run through what they want to do and how they want to do it well before they arrive at the arena. They imagine the sights, sounds, temperatures, spectators, and the other competitors—and then they focus on their own performances. Some even include a clock or stopwatch in their imagery to ensure that the timing and pacing in their minds are exact. To your brain, a dress rehearsal is the opening night performance.

Most importantly, when you visualize yourself, see yourself in the present, as if you are already accomplishing your goal. Make certain your visual image is as you would see it through your own eyes, not watching through the eyes of a spectator. If you're a skier, your imagery would appear in your mind as if an invisible TV camera were mounted on your shoulder looking exactly where your eyes are focused during a ski run and feeling the same sensations. If you need to give a speech, you should imagine exactly how the audience will look sitting in front of you.

When you talk to others, use words that are rich in visual imagery; word pictures, analogies, stories, metaphors, and

similes create vivid mental pictures. You will enjoy a side benefit of becoming a better conversationalist and public speaker if
you do.

Getting in touch with your five senses will greatly enhance
your ability to layer new positive habits over the old ones. Your
imagination has the incredible ability to pre-play and replay
sensory events as if they were really happening at the present
moment. This is a testament to the universal truth that thoughts
become things. Imagination plus repetition creates internalization and, ultimately, realization.

The most important conversations, briefings, meetings, and lectures you will ever have will be those you hold with yourself in the privacy of your own mind.

Learn from the past, set vivid, detailed goals for the future, and live in the only moment of time over which you have any control: NOW.

Chapter 8

Laser Focus:
The Awesome Power of Purpose

FOCUS PRECEDES SUCCESS

No one really has a time management problem. We really have a focus problem. We spend too much energy worrying about the things we want to do but can't, instead of concentrating on doing the things we can do but don't. Dreams are the creative visions of our lives in the future. Dreams are what we would like our lives to become. Goals, on the other hand, are the specific events that we intend to make happen. Goals should be just beyond our present reach, but never out of sight. Think of your goals as previews of coming attractions of an epic, real-life movie in which you are the screenwriter, producer, and star performer. Goals are our method of concentrating energy. By defining what needs to be done within reasonable time limits, we have a way of measuring success.

Laser technology and effective goal achievement are based upon the same scientific principles. When light waves are concentrated and in step they produce a beam of pure light with awesome power. When goals are kept in focus and are approached in orderly progression, they ignite the human mind's awesome creativity and powers of accomplishment. Concentrate your attention on where you want to go, not away from where you don't want to be. You will always move in the direction of your current dominant thoughts.

Think of your mind as a marvelous GPS system, but instead of a Global Positioning Satellite system, either hand held or in our cars, your brain is like a GPS system, where GPS means Goal Positioning System. Tell your internal GPS where you want to go. Be as specific as possible. The more inputs the better. And it will guide you there. But first you must know where you are right now. And where you want to go.

You are the world's greatest expert on yourself. No one knows more about your hopes, your dreams, your fears, and frustrations than you do. In your secret heart, your goals are quite clearly defined, and most likely they have been since your childhood. That doesn't mean, however, that you won't choose to delude yourself about them. All of us feel the pressure of what we believe the world expects us to do and be, and under that pressure most of us feel the need to compromise on what we really want from life. This is part of growing up, and it's inevitable. But the danger arises when we convince ourselves that growing up means not just adjusting, but abandoning what we really want and need. This happens because we spend too much time fantasizing and not enough time prioritizing and internalizing.

Some people believe The Law of Attraction means throwing a dream out into the universe and expecting the universe to respond like the genie in Aladdin's magic lamp. I believe The Law of Attraction takes daily action. Today is a new starting point for your journey.

Questions: What did you love to do as a child? Are you doing what you enjoy now in your personal and professional life and using your talents fully? Are you making a contribution to the world and to other people that gives you a feeling of self-respect? Even if you're not pursuing your childhood aspirations today, it's still important to think back to what you loved to do and what talents you displayed at an early age.

Actions: Identify your personal character strengths, your natural abilities, and educational experiences that may have brought you special knowledge and skills. Make note of the people who are your primary personal network of role models and mentors, who I refer to as "sounding boards" and "springboards" on the road to success.

By journaling these in writing, you can create a detailed self-assessment of where you are today, in relation to your goals. You can give real meaning to the phrase "Back to the Future!" If you don't take a practical approach to achieving your goals, sooner or later you'll start beating yourself up for your pie-in-the-sky dreams and you'll start settling for less than you really want because you don't clearly see how anything more is possible.

While I was a naval officer in Washington, DC after the Korean War, I conducted a study of North Korean and Chinese interrogation methods. These methods were designed to separate and identify any captured Americans who could be turned into collaborators or informers, and I discovered that it had been relatively easy for the captors to separate strong-willed leaders among their prisoners from purposeless followers. The interrogation appeared simple and nonthreatening. Where are you from? Do you have a girlfriend back home? What are you fighting for? What are you going to do when you return home? What kind of career would like most? What are you planning to study? How much money do you need? What is your favorite sports team? What is your religion?

Soldiers and airmen who gave specific, practical answers were classified as goal-oriented, potential leaders. They were placed in maximum-security camps, were deprived of adequate food and shelter, and were tortured in an attempt to break their resolve. But Americans who gave vague answers about their lives and their futures were recognized as ideal subjects for indoctrination, referred to as "brainwashing." They were put in minimum-security camps that were almost like country clubs, with no machine-gun towers, no barbed-wire fences, and no guard dogs. Instead, there were comfortable barracks, cafeterias, and recreation areas. Most importantly, there were study halls for reading and listening to Communist propaganda.

Though the prisoners in the maximum-security camps were beaten, starved, and forced to live in cages like animals, some escaped and got back to friendly territory. In contrast, no one escaped or even attempted to escape from the minimum-security country clubs. And yet, incredibly, despite superior food, shelter, clothing, and medical care, death and disease rates were many times higher than in the maximum-security camps. Having no tangible goals to motivate them in the minimum-security camps, several of our young servicemen pulled the covers up over their heads and died, for no apparent reason other than the absence of a cause for which to live.

If you don't know where you're going, it doesn't make any difference if the alarm clock goes off in the morning. If you don't stand for something, you'll fall for anything. But if your goals are vivid, specific, flexible, and supported by action plans and sub-goals, you'll believe that your life is worth living. And you'll be right!

DELAYED GRATIFICATION

Delayed gratification is perhaps the most difficult concept to teach people in America and the industrialized nations today. But it's really what separates champions from also-rans. It's the reason immigrants are often able to succeed when they arrive in any wealthier country. They're eager to work at doing things that the majority of the population are not willing to consider.

Your definition of success will change throughout your life. Think of success as a lifetime journey, not a destination. Always remember, focus precedes success. One of the major reasons so few people reach their goals is that most people don't set specific goals, and the mind just dismisses them as irrelevant. Most people want financial security but have never considered how much money it will take. Would it surprise you to learn that only five of every one hundred Americans who are in the higher income professions such as law and medicine reach age

65 without having to depend upon government support? I was astounded to learn that so few individuals achieve any degree of financial success regardless of their level of income during their most productive years. Most people live their lives under the delusion that they're immortal in the body. They squander their money and their time and their minds with activities that are tension relieving instead of goal achieving. Many Americans and others—who are not motivated to succeed—work to get through the week with enough extra money to spend on the weekend.

Sometime ago during a live goal setting seminar for executives, we asked the participants to write down and discuss five questions which all centered around their goals. In the goal setting seminars that I've been giving throughout the United States and internationally, it's obvious that the majority of the people spend more time planning a party or a vacation than they do planning their lives. By failing to plan, they are actually planning to fail by default. In one of my early seminars, I divided two hundred participants into groups of six attendees each and they sat at circular tables, and they wrote down and discussed their personal responses to each part in a series of five questions. The questions I asked were these:

1. What are your greatest personal and professional abilities and liabilities?

2. What are your most important personal and professional goals for the balance of this year?

3. What is a major personal and professional goal you have for next year?

4. What will your professional level and annual income be in five years?

5. Twenty years from now, where will you be living, what will you be doing, what will you have accomplished that could be written or said about you by family or peers? What state of health will you enjoy and what will your assets be in dollars?

Well, after the groaning and grumbling had subsided, the master mind groups went to work discussing the most important topics they could ever share. As difficult and unreasonable as these questions may appear, you must remember that these two hundred people each paid $250 to attend a goal setting workshop and they seem dumbfounded that someone actually was challenging them to think about their own lives in specific terms. It was fun to sit and listen to the stories of people crawling out of the ghetto into greatness, but it was no fun to consider doing it yourself. That sounded like work or being back in school.

They struggled trying to be specific, because most of them had work priorities or quotas assigned in their jobs but had never given any definition or priority to their own personal goals. All but one person, who was too young to have given up on his dreams. He was a red-haired, freckle-faced ten-year-old named Eric, who tagged along with his father to get some positive input. Instead, his output startled the adults in the group. When he was asked the five specific questions, he eagerly went down the list. He said his greatest talents were building model airplanes and doing well in computer games. He said he needed improvement in cleaning his room and being nice to his sister. His personal goal for that year was to build a model of the space shuttle and his professional goal was to earn four hundred dollars doing yard work for neighbors. For the following year, his personal goal was to take a trip to Hawaii and his professional goal was to earn seven hundred dollars for the super-saver travel package. When asked about his five-year goals, he said: "I'll be fifteen in the tenth grade, and I'll be taking a lot of math, science, and computer classes."

Eric had to think for a moment when asked about his twenty-year life goals. He said, "Twenty years from now, I'll be thirty years old, right? I'll be living in Cape Kennedy, Florida as a space-shuttle astronaut working for NASA. I'll be in great physical shape. You have to be in good shape and study hard to be an astronaut," he finished proudly.

Just boyhood fantasies, you might think? Eric graduated from the Air Force Academy, entered flight training, and on his thirty-first birthday, he celebrated in outer space aboard the space shuttle, putting a communication satellite into orbit.

Question: How much money will you need to save so that you can live the quality of life you desire without going to work every day?

Action: Begin paying your "future" as the first mandatory expense out of your weekly or monthly take-home pay. It should be at least 10 percent.

The previous action idea, in which you were you were asked to define the amount of money that will give you a comfortable residual income without having to work is such an important question, we should cover it in more depth.

Many people love money, because it gives them the appearance of superiority, which, of course, is only a mirage, since money can't purchase respect, the love of a child, or another moment of life. What has always puzzled me is that many celebrities talk about the injustices suffered by the oppressed only after they have pocketed millions themselves. The truth is money is fuel. It's your mentality and motivation that count.

Wealth provides freedom and independence; it releases you from the petty problems and tyranny of the small stuff in life, like car problems, orthodontics, home repairs, and so forth. Wealth, when earned, builds the character of personal achievement. It is concrete evidence of accomplishment which builds self-respect. Wealth helps you live your life without as much fear of catastrophic loss. You can risk pursuing your dreams more. Wealth gives you more control over your daily life. You can go where, with whom, and when you want, and pay your bills as you go. Wealth enables you to support causes you believe in, in a material way, and can be distributed to others who need and deserve your help.

Most people live the so-called golden years in near-poverty, depending on state and federal agencies, or their relatives, for their survival needs. Retirement, for most people, means being cast aside and no longer relevant. The problem is, because of medical intervention, we are living a lot longer than we can afford to, and the quality doesn't usually match the quantity. Make it your goal to live as long as you can with both the health and wealth abundance mentality. Do you deserve to enjoy wealth? You bet you do. You owe it to yourself and loved ones.

DEFINE WHAT FINANCIAL SECURITY MEANS TO YOU

Financial security is the value you place on the time of your life. You need to define the quality of life you're seeking first, and then compute how much it's going to cost to finance that quality, with a standard of living that can be maintained without continuing your current employment. That's the bottom line.

In your mind, picture your life as a stairway you are walking down, with five steps to fulfillment. Instead of an uphill climb, view it as a downhill hike, walking carefully and surely. Complete this picture by placing five large empty buckets on each of the five steps and label them from the top bucket to the bottom: Survival, Stability, Quality, Security, and Independence. This is what I call the "Overflowing Buckets Concept" of creating financial independence. It's like Abraham Maslow's hierarchy of needs by putting first things first in their order of importance.

The object is to fill each of the five buckets full of dollars as you progress down the stairway, so that when one bucket overflows, it spills into the next bucket down on the next step.

Bucket One, the Survival Bucket, is how you budget your basic needs of food, shelter, and basic existence. Over your cost of living, any extra money flows into Bucket Two, which is the Stability Bucket. Financial stability is the ability to remain solvent in the event of sudden, unforeseen changes and emergencies in your life. It is called insurance against catastrophic loss. It means having an emergency fund in a savings account equal to a minimum of three months' income, preferably six months' income. It includes having adequate medical insurance and life insurance that remains in force regardless of your employment status, that is permanent and transferable.

One of the greatest financial blunders most people make is to assume that insurance against premature death is all they need, besides health, home, and auto insurance. The likelihood of loss of income due to injury or illness is much greater than loss of life. Not only are you without income when you are sick or injured, you also need to be cared for and the expenses continue to mount even though you're not able to work.

The next bucket you need to start filling after Survival and Stability is the Quality of Life Bucket. This is where you sit down with significant others and determine what standard of living will give you the quality of life you desire—the home, possessions, education for children, recreation, and vacation. These items should be budgeted and saved for, rather than put on credit cards.

Once you have established a savings habit for your quality of life, a little discretionary income should also be set aside for bucket four. This is the Financial Security Bucket. Financial security is defined as the amount of assets in dollars that will give you the amount of monthly income you need for the quality of life you desire, at some pre-determined point in the future, without having to depend upon day-to-day employment. Less than 5 percent of Americans ever fill this bucket. Your goal is to be in the top five percent who do. To get in the top five percent club, you need to put about 10 percent of your spendable income into an appreciating investment fund at the first of every month, like a utility bill or mortgage payment. Treat it as the most urgent bill you need to pay.

The fifth and final bucket at the bottom of the stairs is Personal Freedom or Financial Independence. This is achieved when you beat the target date you set for retirement. Personal freedom is when work is a choice not a necessity; when you can do what you want, when you want, and your health and energy levels enable you to do virtually anything you desire. Being free to chase your passion, not your pension is one of the greatest goals you can set and reach.

FIVE POWERS OF EFFECTIVE GOAL SETTING

Here are five "powers" that will help you create more focused goals to achieve your dreams:

The Power of the Positive. Your goals should be framed in positive terms. Winners dwell on the rewards of success, while losers dwell on the penalties of failure. In other words, instead of focusing on "not being late," "not being fat," "not being in debt," or "not working in my regular job," you want to concentrate on images of achievement, such as "I'm an on-time person." "I am lean and am in great shape." "I am creating wealth and success in my business." Remember that your mind cannot concentrate on the reverse of an idea, so keep your goals framed in the positive.

The Power of the Present. Your character goals, such as being a good leader, parent, or being healthy, on-time, enthusiastic, for example, should be framed as images of achievement in the present tense. Your long-term memory stores information in real time, that is critically important to you. The reason your memory stores information in the present tense is obvious. Can you imagine what would happen if your mind had to remind your heart to beat tomorrow? Or what if it put the command for breathing, eating, or calorie burning on next month's agenda? So any goal that involves your health, behavior, or self-leadership should be framed as if you are already that person. Some examples might include: "I spend quality time with my loved ones." "I am always on time for meetings." "I am feeling healthier every day." "I have healthy habits that add years to my life and life to my years." "I am relaxed and in control." "I encourage input and ideas from the employees I lead."

The Power of the Personal. I cannot stress this enough. Your images of achievement must be yours. They cannot be your boss's goals, your spouse's goals, or your friend's goals. No goal set for you by others will ever be sought with the same passion, effort, commitment, or motivation as the one you set for yourself. Keep your mind focused on your own goals but achieve them by helping others succeed.

Questions: What does winning really mean to me? What does being successful mean to me? What do I really want to achieve in my life in the long run? What are my talents and capabilities? What am I willing to sacrifice, trade off, or invest in to become more successful? And how will other people benefit from my success? How will my life be improved by my success? How will my life be complicated by my success? And who can I count on to nurture and support me in my pursuits?

Actions: Remember, personal goals, the ones you want, are those you'll be more likely to achieve. And when you do set personal, meaningful goals, keep them to yourself. Or share them only with other winners who will take the time to give you positive feedback and input. Remember, misery is always looking for a place to become company. Never share a dream with someone who's likely to rain on your parade.

The Power of Precision. Make your images of achievement specific and precise. Remember when you talk about goals in generalities, you will very rarely succeed. But when you talk about your goals with specificity, you will very rarely fail.

Question: A good way for you to determine if your images of achievement are focused enough is to simply ask yourself, "Can this goal be timed, checked, or measured?"

Action: Set a due date in writing for each of your major goals. You may want to break your long-range goals into incremental sub-goals of about 90 days for completion.

If you cannot time, check, or measure your performance, your goals are not specific enough. Your brain is more marvelous than any computer that will ever be invented. Think of your brain and central nervous system as the hardware, and your mind as the software program. The mind does not compute ideas like "doing your best," "doing better," "getting rich," "being happy," or "having enough." It deals only with specificity, not vague ideas. What are your income needs for next year? What is your desired weight? What amount of cash asset do you need to save, that will give you enough income to enjoy your life in the future, after taxes, without depending upon employment? At what age do you plan to be financially secure? The brain and mind respond to specifics, like spending seven-tenths of your take-home pay on current living expenses. Spending two-tenths of your take-home pay on reducing your debts. And putting at least one-tenth of your take-home pay in a mutual fund, or interest bearing savings vehicle to finance your future. Make it your mission focus on specific achievements. Change masters concentrate their energy. They have detailed, magnificent obsessions. They have laser focus and will tolerate little distraction away from their goals.

The Power of the Possible. A formula that works well is that your goals should be just out of reach but not out of sight. Another way to state that is that your goals should be realistic, but not achievable by ordinary means. Your goals should also be broken down into small, incremental action steps. Remember the best way to eat an elephant is one bite at a time. So set challenging, realistic goals with small, doable action steps. It's always useful to clarify long range goals, the ones that have been stimulating future benefits that are worth the wait and the work. Long range goals, however, don't offer you the step-by-step reinforcement and feedback you need for continued motivation. So, if possible, break your long range goals into many short range ones where you can know the thrill of victory on a smaller scale. Then you can thrive on the many smaller wins spaced closer together, which will give you a winning pattern that will strengthen you for the long haul toward the bigger long range goals.

The idea is to set short-term goals that are just beyond your current range of skills. And when you miss one of these short-term increments, you review, revise, and retry. When you hit your incremental goal, you reinforce yourself with a positive reward or ceremony. Face the challenge, meet it, or learn from your mistakes and then move up to the next higher goal. The point is, we all need to win and win again to develop the winning reflex. Setting step-by-step goals that can be reach, revised, retried, and reinforced really works.

It seems to be an irrevocable part of nature that we work harder toward our goals as our deadlines approach. A material goal is not a goal unless it has a deadline. That's why we have quotas, due dates, quarterly reports, and dates for exams and term papers in school. We humans work best when we have a target date for arrival and the best goals are in writing that we can review on a daily basis. Attorneys know the wisdom of the written contract. It demands clarity, specificity, conditions, a time frame, and commitment of money. When all the terms are understood and mutually agreed upon, it usually results in better performance. Before you leave your place of business in the evening, write down at least five personal goals you want to reach the following day. Before you go to sleep that night prioritize these five personal goals and focus on how you'll start reaching them the next morning.

Question: Do your goals pass the win-win test? To be true winners for life we must consider the impact of reaching our goals on other people. Once a goal is defined as to its integrity and merit for our own success, we must ask ourselves the key question before we embark on an action course. "What affect will the realization of my goal have on the others involved?" And the answer should be beneficial. One of the most critical aspects of goal setting is that we seldom succeed in isolation without the support of others. When our own goals match the aspirations of those with whom we come in frequent contact and they in turn identify with us, a chain reaction is formed and the whole is greater than the sum of its parts. Synergy is achieved when a team is striving for the same outcome.

Think of your own dreams and goals as previews of coming attractions in your life, in which you are the producer, scriptwriter, and star performer in an exciting documentary. Remember, focus always precedes success. The mind cannot begin to formulate the strategies and actions required without specific information. Your mind will simply not respond to a request to get rich, have more, do better, or make money. Once you set a goal, you can adjust and fine tune it any way you wish. That's creativity. And persistence is what allows you to keep progressing toward the goal no matter how many adjustments are required, and no matter how long it takes to accomplish it. After more than forty years of research, we've discovered that the main reason individuals fail to reach their goals is that they never really set them properly in the first place. The brain and mind are target seeking by design.

Action: Concentrate your attention on where you want to go, not away from where you don't want to be. You will always move in the direction of your current dominant thoughts. What you see is who you'll be and what you set is what you'll get.

At the beginning of this chapter we asked you to think of your mind as a marvelous GPS system, but instead of a Global Positioning System, either hand held or in your car, your brain can be compared to a Goal Positioning System. Tell your internal GPS where you want to go, as specific as possible, and it will guide you there. But first you must know where you are right now, and with vivid clarity as to where you want to go.

When goals are kept in focus and are approached in orderly progression, they ignite the human brain's awesome power of accomplishment like a laser. We spend too much energy worrying about the things we want to do but can't, instead of concentrating on the things we can do but don't. I certainly don't embrace a formula approach to goal setting and believe in opening our minds to the vast potential within, which offers amazing opportunities to all who dare to dream big and think outside the box. I believe in unleashing our imaginations to dream as globally and boldly as possible, with no restrictions. However, having worked extensively with astronauts, entrepreneurs, and world-class athletes, I also believe strongly in focused action and stair-stepping our way to the top of every mountain we hope to climb with discipline, training, and perseverance.

Goals should always be the means, not the end. Goals are like stepping-stones to the stars. In my work with top athletes whose goal was to win a gold medal or a world championship,

I have observed that once they reached that pinnacle, they had nowhere to go. Can you imagine reaching your ultimate goal before you were twenty-five or thirty years of age? Or, in the case of many Olympians, before you were twenty?

Nor is this syndrome limited to sports stars. I know a business executive whose major goal was to become financially independent by the age of forty and then retire to play golf. He reached that goal but became extremely bored after a year of playing golf every day. Fortunately, he recognized the problem and found a solution. He went back to college, earned a degree in a completely different field, and today is happily engaged in a new career as an environmental engineer.

Traditionally, many people have had a goal of "lifetime security" in a permanent job. Today, with technology changing how we work and live minute by minute, that is virtually impossible. Even government and military service is vulnerable. Instead of aspiring to lifetime security, it is better to focus on being well qualified in as many areas as possible for a challenging, ever evolving career. Staying well qualified means ensuring that goals don't become dead ends or stopping points. It means being able to set new standards when you achieve your current goals.

As you meet and even exceed your goals, you must learn to balance two distinct but important elements of a fulfilling life. First, it's important to take satisfaction in your achievements, to enjoy your success, and to "smell the roses" every day. But it's just as important to remember that the real joy of achievement is in the challenge, not in the accomplishment. Even in a rapidly changing world, the wisdom of the ages never changes: "The road to heaven is heaven itself."

Golda Meir, a former prime minister of Israel, was known for her vision and wisdom. She was a shopkeeper's daughter, as was Margaret Thatcher, a former prime minister of the United Kingdom. She attended school in the fortress-like building on Fourth Street near Milwaukee's famous Schlitz brewing factory. Speaking only broken English after immigrating from Europe, this plain, nondescript child was late for school almost every day because of the chores she had to do at home. But brilliant, courageous, and persistent, she became one of the most respected world leaders of the twentieth century.

At the age of seventy-one, while serving as prime minister, she returned to Milwaukee and her school. It had been fifty-one years since she had left the United States. She told the inner city youth at her old school that she had been born into a minority environment and had lived only slightly above the poverty level. She also told the children, "When you're young, it isn't really important to decide exactly what you want to become when you grow up. It is much more important to decide on the way you want to live." Golda Meir spoke of service rather than material reward, and of destiny rather than money.

I know several top executives who own fabulous homes in the country and by the ocean, but they go home only to eat and sleep. They've worked hard to have those vistas outside their windows, but they rarely enjoy them. The longer Japanese executives stay at the office, and the more pressure they place on themselves, the more they are held in esteem by their companies. The Japanese call their living conditions *manuke*, which means "we lack three things—time, space, and private lives."

While I am very much in favor of time freedom and quality of life, I see little point in outward trappings to proclaim, "I've arrived!" to the world. Oscar Wilde once defined a cynic as "someone who knows the price of everything and the value of nothing."

The true value of a person is measured by lasting contribution to the general good. It's interesting to note that the largest gifts to sponsor the world's greatest museums, fine arts, and performing arts centers, and many of our finest universities and medical schools, have come from anonymous donors.

Ask yourself: How fast am I spending my time and energy? On what am I spending them? Will this problem or effort really matter in five, ten, or fifty years? Most importantly, is this activity moving me toward my life-forming passions?

Chase your passion, not your pension.

Habits are like submarines. They run silent and deep.

Chapter 9

The New Brain Train:
Rewiring Your Habit Patterns

REPETITION LEADS TO INTERNALIZATION

We learn by observation, imitation, and repetition. We observe role models and others. We imitate their behavior. We repeat that behavior until it is internalized like brushing our teeth or driving our cars. Observation, imitation, repetition, internalization. Why do we do what we do, when we know what we know? Because we do what we have learned, even though we know better. Some people smoke, although they know it is very detrimental to health. Much of what we have learned is by imitation. First, we observe the behaviors of relatives, friends, or role models. Then we imitate that behavior. Then we repeat and internalize the behavior, and the idea, notion, act, or belief grows layer upon layer from a flimsy cobweb into an unbreakable cable to strengthen or shackle our lives.

It's amazing how parents continue to pass their own hang-ups on to their children. It reminds me of the story about the young bride who cooked a ham for her new husband. Before putting it in the pan, she cut off both ends. When her husband asked her why she did that, she replied that her mother had always done it that way. At a later date, when they were having baked ham dinner at her mother's home, he asked her, casually, why she cut both ends off the ham. The mother shrugged and said she really didn't know, except that her mother had always done it that way. Finally, he asked the grandmother why she always cut the ends off the ham before she baked it. She looked at him suspiciously, replying, "Because my baking dish is too small!"

Do you recognize this autobiography?

> You may know me. I'm your constant companion. I'm your greatest helper. I'm your heaviest burden. I'll push you onward or drag you down to failure. I'm at your command. Half the tasks you do might as well be turned over to me. I'm able to do them quickly, and I'm able to do them the same every time, if that's what you want. I'm easily managed. All you've got to do is be firm with me. Show me exactly how you want it done, and after a few lessons, I'll do it automatically. I'm the servant of all great men and women, and of course, the servant of all the failures, as well. I've made all the great winners who've ever been great, and I've made all the losers, too. But I work with all the precision of a marvelous computer with the intelligence of a human being. You may run me for profit, or you

may run me to ruin. It makes no difference to me. Take me! Be easy with me, and I'll destroy you. Be firm with me, and I'll put the world at your feet. Who am I? Why, I'm Habit.

The force of habit is your greatest tool for success. We all first make our habits; then our habits make us. Habits are like submarines; they run silent and deep. The chains of our habits are usually too small to be recognized until they're too strong to be broken. When we begin to deal with the attitudes and actions that bind us, we give ourselves permission to take control and to build new habit patterns that help us perform to our ultimate potential. There is a critical difference between knowing something and learning how to make it a part of our everyday game plan. The secret is repetition, repetition, repetition. Repetition creates habit. Habit becomes conviction. Conviction controls action. Right now in this instant, you're engaged in one of the best habits of all: that of experiencing information that will benefit you rather than frustrate and defeat you.

While our brains receive thousands of inputs each day, it seems that we lock in most aggressively on those that are negative. But the good news is you can change your life by changing your mindset and, over time, create new habits. Psychologists have now done scores of scientifically validated studies to find how habits are formed. We now know how to track a habit from the time the sensory nerves carry the message from our hearing, touch, vision, taste, and smell to the data-processing areas of our brains. The brain then makes a decision, based on this information, and immediately sends the working order through the motor nerves to the appropriate parts of the body demanding action.

It should then come as no surprise that after the body responds in the same way to identical stimuli a number of times, a habit is being formed. And here is the most interesting part. Because of this repetition, the message from the sensory nerve learns to jump over to the conditioned motor nerve without a conscious decision by the brain. Think about it. Reframing your thoughts and actions repeatedly—and layer upon layer—new neural pathways are formed, which can be likened to new software programs installed in the hard drive of our computers. We don't think about it; we just run the program.

While it seems more difficult to replace a bad habit with a good one, the development of good habits enjoys the same sequencing. It depends on input, practice, and supporting environment. For a habit to become a permanent part of your life, it can take about a year of committed practice to firmly internalize it and possibly longer for it to override your past experiences and former bad habits that have been developed over a lifetime. We are all wired differently, with each individual's physiology unique to that person, and, therefore, timeframes for successful habit change vary from being ingrained after three months to nearly a year of continual daily activity.

Sometimes you've got to stop and take a look at where you've been:

Checking out your closets and the stuff you're tossing in.

Looking in your freezer at the pizzas and the meat.

Going through your cupboards counting everything that's sweet.

Getting on the bathroom scale you see the extra weight

And realize that every pound was on your dinner plate;

You're staring in the mirror trying not to get upset,

But you're looking at a stranger you wish you'd never met!

When I was young I had the habit of always being late,

I guess that's why my name is mostly W-A-I-T, wait.

Now I practice what I preach, coming early for each date

And now I'm known to be the one who's first at every gate.

Habits are reflexes that grow inside your brain.

You can change the flow of traffic by the way you think and train.

Repetition is the key to leave unhealthy ways behind.

You can reset your life and live it if you'll just reset your mind.

Think of your brain as a complex series of highways, over-passes, and side streets. When you drive to and from work, or from your home to the store, you take the same route over and over again. It becomes second nature. The recent breakthroughs in neuroscience have shown that you can build new freeways and short-cuts in your brain to take you to new destinations that you may never have considered before. The unfamiliar becomes familiar. The roadblocks become overpasses. The dead ends become freeways.

Your perceptions are your realities. Whether you are aware of it or not, your world is actually a virtual world based upon first- and secondhand experiences, beliefs, prejudices, misconceptions, facts, fads, fallacies, and timeless truth. People's decisions are first influenced by emotional triggers, and then by logic. Emotions dominate the decision-making process. People have far less access to their own mental activities than perceived. About 95 percent of thinking is an unconscious, habitual process. People's memories do not accurately represent their experiences. People's memories are constantly changing without their awareness. Instead of a Facebook photo album, memory is more like a constantly edited music video, full of fragments, real and imagined. As you are remembering something, your brain is in the process of "rewiring" the connections between neurons, which is actually changing the structure of your brain. Rather than video playback, your memory is more like video editing. Every time you remember something you are changing, recreating, or re-memorizing. A memory is subject to change every time you remember it. The ability to rewire your brain to generate success and health-related pathways is at the forefront of individual and team peak performance.

Question: What is one unhealthy or undesirable habit you would like to change?

Action: Be willing to begin practicing a replacement habit and stay with it for six months to a year. By doing that, it will become as automatic as brushing your teeth or driving your car.

THE FOUR CORNERSTONES OF CHANGE

Habits, like comfortable beds, are easy to fall into, but hard to get out of. If we won't master our habits, our habits will master us. When we allow unhealthy habits to be our guide and counsel, we give up control of our actions, and find ourselves at the mercy of that blind giant who calls the shots without any concern for our well-being. However, when we begin to deal with the attitudes and actions that bind us, we give ourselves permission to take control and to build new habit patterns that help us perform to our ultimate potential. There are four ideas that we call the Four Cornerstones of Change. Understanding these four concepts will help you understand the right way to develop healthy habits.

Cornerstone #1: No one else can change you. You must first admit the need for change, give up any denial of your role in the problem, and take full responsibility for changing yourself. You must also understand that you can't change anyone else, either. You can influence and inspire others as a mentor, but they, as individuals, are ultimately responsible for gaining new inputs, practicing them, and surrounding themselves with a team of positive supporters.

Cornerstone #2: Habits are not easily broken; they are replaced by layering new behavior patterns on top of the old ones over time. Since many habits have been internalized for years, it's foolish to assume that three or four weeks of training will override the old, destructive patterns. To change any habits, including substance abuse, self-ridicule, eating disorders, and any other destructive lifestyles, forget about the 30-day wonder cures, the 60-day diet delights, and the get-fit, get-rich-quick fads. Give yourself about a year to internalize permanent change. Be patient. It took a number of years and observation, imitation, and repetition for you to pick up and store your current habits.

Cornerstone #3: A daily routine adhered to over time will become second nature, like brushing your teeth or driving your car. Continue to practice your mistakes on the golf driving range, and you'll remain a high-handicap duffer. Learn from a professional, and then practice the correct swing with each club as demonstrated by the pro, and you'll become the pride of your foursome.

My favorite true story is about United States Air Force Colonel George Hall. He was a pilot who was shot down and parachuted into enemy territory. Five and a half years in solitary confinement in a prisoner of war camp. In his cell alone, in black pajamas and bare feet, pacing in his cell for five and a half years, with no light, no talking to other prisoners, and one plate of rice each day.

To keep his sanity and pass the time, he decided to play golf in his imagination. You see, he had been a four handicap golfer, averaging about 76 strokes per 18 holes, before he was captured. He played one round of golf in his mind every day for five and a half years. He put an invisible ball on the tee and drove the ball down the fairway. He used his other clubs and irons to reach the green. He measured the putts going through the motions of pulling the flag out and watched his ball go in the cup. For five and a half years, he replayed every game he'd ever played well. He also pre-played every game he'd only seen the pros play on television. Pre-play and replay. After five and a half years, he became atrophied, and his eyesight weakened. And he was withered and underweight. And he came back and went to the New Orleans PGA Open and shot a 76. Four over par matching his former handicap. But he had not played on a real golf course in nearly six years. And the media said, "Wow! Congratulations, Colonel! Beginners re-entry luck?" He said, "Luck? Are you kidding? I never three-putted a green in five and a-half years."

And, they said, "Sir, did you have a golf course at the POW camp?" He said, "Yeah, in a way. We all have one. In your imagination, you never miss." In the POW camp he was doing within while he was doing without.

Many people have defined self-discipline as doing without. But a better definition of self-discipline is doing within while you're doing without. Self-discipline is no more than mental practice, the commitment to memory of those thoughts, emotions, and daily actions that will override current information stored in the subconscious memory bank. Then, through relentless repetition, the penetration of these new inputs into our subconscious results in the creation of a new self-image.

So, you have this ability to set up in advance what you want. And, when you don't make it, you correct it. When you do make it, you confirm it. Practice makes permanent. Practicing negative behaviors leads to a losing lifestyle. Practicing positive behaviors leads to a winning lifestyle. It's so obvious that it's often completely overlooked, especially by the entertainment and news media, who help form our basic opinions on how the world works.

And Cornerstone #4: Once you change a habit, stay away from the old, destructive environment. The reason most criminals return to prison is that they make the mistake of returning to their old neighborhoods and their old friends when they're paroled the first time. No matter how much they regret their actions while in prison and want to go straight, they're easily dragged back into their old ways by exposure to the negative environment. When dieters reach their desired weight, they usually go back to their former eating routines because their new behavior patterns haven't been imbedded long enough to make them strong enough to pass by the dessert section of the buffet. Overweight individuals and dieters should stay away from buffet lines.

When our mind talks, our body listens and acts accordingly. We need to understand there is a victor's behavioral circle. Our self-image determines our practice. How we practice determines our performance and that instantaneously, immediately after every performance, we engage in self-talk in words, pictures, and emotions to confirm or adjust our self-image about that particular action. It's a cycle. It's a cycle up or a cycle down. And the self-talk we use after every performance determines whether the new self-image will reinforce the win or reinforce the loss.

Question: How often do you engage in negative self-talk or self-criticism?

Action: For one full day, from awakening until sleeping, write down the number of times you are critical of yourself and/ or others. When you become aware of this habit, say to yourself: "Stop, bad seeds. That's not like me. I'm better than that."

YOUR SILENT CONVERSATIONS

Our brains respond more intensely to images and emotions than they do to verbal commands. However, words also cause automatic emotional reactions and autonomic physiological responses. Verbal abuse can be as devastating as physical abuse. When your brain talks, your body listens and acts accordingly. Research has shown that our thoughts can raise and lower body temperature, secrete hormones, relax muscles and nerve endings, dilate and constrict arteries, and raise and lower pulse rate. With this evidence, it is obvious that we need to control the language we use on ourselves. Neuroscience has proven that repeated mental practice can help rewire our brains to create new, positive habits.

Winners rarely put themselves down in words before or after a performance; they use positive feed-forward self-talk and positive feedback self-talk as part of their training programs until it becomes a force of habit. They say, "I can…," "I will…," "Next time I'll get it right," "I'm feeling better," "I'm ready," "Thank you." Losers fall into the trap of saying, "I can't…," "I'm a klutz," "I can't stay in shape," "I wish…," "If only…," "I should have…," "Yeah, but…."

You are your most important critic. There is no opinion as vitally important to your success, fitness, and well-being as the opinion you have of yourself. The most important meetings, briefings, coaching sessions, and conversations you'll ever have are the conversations you will have with yourself. As you read this, you're talking to yourself: "Let's see if I understand what they mean by that. How does that compare with my own experiences? I already knew that...I think I'll try that."

We believe that this self-talk, this psycholinguistics or language of the mind, is critical to our success and can be controlled to work for us in achieving our goals of health, performance, and longevity. We're all talking to ourselves every moment of our lives, except during certain portions of our sleeping cycle. It comes automatically. We're seldom even aware that we're doing it. We all have a running commentary going on in our heads on events and our reactions to them.

Current neurological and psychological research confirms the incredible ability of the mind to drive the body to achieve the individual's immediate dominant thought by instructing the body to carry out the vivid images of performance as if they had been achieved before and are merely being repeated. With pre-play simulation (or feed-forward) you can engrave in your mind the verbal, visual, and emotional conditions associated with high performance, good health, and long life. This process greatly influences your daily habit patterns and acts as a steering program toward your goals. With replay simulation (or feedback) you can replay your successes during quiet times or off days to reinforce your self-confidence in stressful times. The feedback also allows you to enter new, positive, corrective data into your thoughts so that you can reset your aim on goals that were previously missed.

Since most of the negative kinds of feelings, beliefs, and attitudes we have about ourselves are stored, through habitual repetition, we need to start relaxing and using self-talk that is constructive and complimentary, instead of destructive and derogatory. Don't let the technique of positive self-talk give you the false impression that you are brainwashing or kidding yourself. On the contrary, we are suggesting just the opposite. We are unconsciously being brainwashed by the television shows and movies we watch, by the lyrics we listen to, and by the people we talk to. Isn't it time we concentrated on information designed for our success rather than our distress? There is little difference between champions and the rest of the pack. The little difference is attitude, and the big difference is whether your attitude is positive or negative. When you talk to yourself, talk yourself up!

Think of where you want to be, and you'll move toward that thought. Self-imaging is what Olympic athletes, actors, and astronauts do. You will recall in Chapter 7 that we mentioned how Olympian Michael Phelps visualizes his performance in advance of his competitive swimming meets. And renowned Olympic gold medalist and World Cup skiing champion Lindsey Vonn says her mental practice gives her a competitive advantage on the course. She says, "I always visualize the run before I do it. By the time I get to the start gate, I've skied that race 100 times already in my head, picturing how I'll take the turns."

Andre Agassi, former World #1 tennis player and eight-time Grand Slam champion, has related how mental practice before a match has helped him throughout his career. Tennis is one of the most solitary of all sports, where the player is alone in his or her head, without the benefit of a coach, caddie, or corner man, for an average of three and a half hours. Agassi reports to using a 22-minute afternoon shower to work on his self-talk, saying things to himself, over and over, until he believes them. He says, "I've won 869 matches in my career, fifth on the all-time list, and many of them were won during the afternoon shower!"

In our previous research with astronauts, executives, and other individuals functioning under pressure, and in our continuing observation of Olympic athletes and high achievers in virtually every profession throughout the world, there is a technique of "scripting" self-talk that seems to be the most effective. The Olympic athletes call this technique the self-statement or image of achievement. Psychologists and psychiatrists call it cognitive reconstruction, or the practice of reframing by internalizing positive thoughts.

There are three basic types of self-statements:

1. General self-talk. These are affirmative statements that can be used at any time and place for a feeling of general well-being. Examples:

"I like myself." "I'm glad I'm me." "I'm relaxing now. I am at peace." "I'm in control of my body." "I feel that my body is healthier now." "I give the best of me in everything." "I am strong and full of energy." "I respect and appreciate myself." "I'm a winner."

2. Specific self-talk. These statements are used to project and reframe, as well as reaffirm, our specific skills, goals, and attributes.

Examples: "I am a team player." "I create value in everything I do."

For a woman, it could be: "I weigh 125 pounds and feel trim in my bathing suit." For a man, it might be. "I feel healthy at my best weight of 175."

"I drink a glass of water with every meal." "I arrive for appointments on time." "I am calm and confident when I take an exam." "I appreciate others' opinions."

"I eat fish or poultry to get my lean protein." "I speak with authority in front of a group."

3. Process self-talk. These are one-word or two-word self-statements that can be used as "trigger" ideas at mealtime, during an exercise workout, or during the performance of professional, sporting, or other demanding skills. Examples:

"Concentrate." "Focus." "Backhand follow-through." "Easy." "Push-off." "Relax." "Let's go."

Your self-talk before a performance will pre-play a positive self-image about specific activities in your life. Your performance will improve because of your elevated self-image, and sometimes your performance will exceed your expectations. Your feedback self-talk will say, "Good for me, now we're getting somewhere." On occasion your performance will fall short of your expectations. Your feedback self-talk will say, "Next time we'll do better. Let's make a target correction to help get it right."

One of the secrets of success is that our responses to our performances—in words, images, and feelings—are just as important as our self-images or simulations of ourselves before we ever attempt to perform in the first place. The vicious cycle is created by negative anticipation, and a negative response to what happens in your daily life. The victor's circle is created by positive anticipation to what is going to happen in your daily life, and a positive reaction no matter what happens. It's not what happens that means the most. It is how you take it and what you make of it, so that next time it will be better.

In order for these self-statements to be most effective, it is extremely important to construct and phrase them properly. Here are specific guidelines for you to use in developing self-talk skills to strengthen your eating habits, your exercise habits, your mental habits, and your professional and personal lifestyle.

1. Make the decision to turn negative self-talk into positive affirmations. Listen to what you are saying and thinking in anticipation of and in response to your daily challenges. Become aware of your own negative self-talk and construct affirmative self-talk statements in their place.

Use positive explanatory statements concerning your professional and personal goals, health, and daily experiences. Pessimists rarely inspire themselves or others to win.

2. Respond rather than react to the negative self-talk of others. The next time someone offers you some of his or her negative statements, don't agree mentally. You can learn either to ignore the comment and say nothing or turn it around and help that person with your positive response to the comment.

3. Direct your self-talk toward what you desire instead of trying to come away from what you don't want. Your mind can't concentrate on the reverse of an idea. If you try to tell yourself not to repeat mistakes, your mind will reinforce the mistake. You want to focus your current dominant thought on your desires, not your dislikes. This is critically important.

Ineffective: "I can quit smoking."

"I'm too fat and have to lose weight."

"I won't be late anymore."

"I won't yell at the children."

Effective: "I am in control of my habits."

"I weigh a slim, trim 125 pounds."

Or for a man, "I feel healthy at 175."

"I arrive early for appointments."

"I am patient and loving with my children."

4. Always use personal pronouns. Words such as I, my, and me will personalize your statements and make them easier to internalize.

Ineffective: "Jogging is good exercise."

Effective: "I enjoy jogging three times a week."

5. Keep your self-talk in the present tense. Referring to the past or future may be counterproductive to making progress.

Ineffective: "Someday I'll get in good physical condition. "

Effective: "I enjoy good health and physical fitness."

Ineffective: "I won't lose those sales again."

Effective: "I gain and retain loyal customers."

6. Keep your self-talk non-competitive instead of measuring yourself against others.

Ineffective: "I will beat John out of the starting position."

Effective: "I am starting on the team and doing the job well."

7. In writing your statements, concentrate on incremental improvement over your previous performance. Don't strive for perfection or unrealistic, superhuman efforts.

Ineffective: "I am the club champion every year."

Effective: "The more I practice the right swing, the better I get."

Once you have correctly constructed images of achievement in the form of self-statements for your goals, write these statements in a journal or smartphone, or record them in your own voice on a laptop, tablet, or hand-held device. Read or listen to the statements at the beginning of your normal routine; get to know them during the day and review them again before you retire at night. Visualize yourself as having already reached each goal you are simulating. Allow yourself actually to feel the pride in doing well. You should be your own coach, mentor, and best friend, since you spend more time with you than with anyone one else. And remember, you will be training your brain into new pathways toward high achievement and fulfillment!

And, the same techniques of mental self-discipline apply to the employee and entrepreneur, as well as the actor and athlete. For example, before a marketing presentation, one successful businessman we know practices in his mind what he'll say and how he'll say it. He imagines what some of the obstacles will be. He focuses on the possible objections and questions his clients may have. And he rehearses how he will overcome them. He sees himself being relaxed, confident, and in good humor. He sees the client satisfied in advance. Now, he may have preferred to go bowling the night before his presentation, but he practices self-discipline by staying home to spend a quiet evening rehearsing the day to come.

The greatest coaches of the greatest teams, the greatest parents of the greatest kids, and the greatest leaders of the greatest companies and countries use the same basic techniques. Explanation, demonstration, correction, repetition, and affirmation. Remember the idea is to replace habits, not to try to erase them. You can't always practice in person, on the field, in the office, with a client, or before the boss. But you can rehearse in your mind, and when your mind talks, your body does listen. Here are some definite action steps that you can take to reinforce the victor's circle in your professional and in your personal life:

1. When you visualize yourself in the present, as if you were already accomplishing one of your goals, make certain that your visual image is as you would see it out of your own eyes and not watching you do it through the eyes of a spectator.

2. If you failed the first time, try again. If you fail a second time, get more feedback as to why you failed. And, if you fail the third time, your sights might be too high for now, so bring your goals in just a little bit from the horizon.

3. Don't scold or berate yourself with left brain criticism when you make a mistake. Develop an affirmative statement about five words in length describing your current performance in the present tense. And relax and listen to yourself state the affirmation and visualize the accompanying action and feeling.

4. And, finally, use positive self-talk from morning to bedtime. It's another good day for me. Things usually work out my way. I expect a great year. Next time, I'll do better. We're going to make it. I'm a winner.

All pursuits begin with an idea of what is to be accomplished or attained. An image of achievement is a tool that permits us to provide accurately encoded information to the brain, so that the mind can work with that information and can begin sharpening perceptions and marshaling resources toward the imagined goal. What we need most in life is continuing support and reinforcement of other winners with similar goals. Every week, meet before work, after work, or during lunch with one or more role models. Form a network with other success-conscious associates in your local community. In everything you do, think, speak, act, behave, and get the habit of success by association. Your mind and body can't distinguish rehearsal from the main event. It stores as reality whatever you practice. You become that to which you are most exposed. Constantly expose yourself to successful individuals, whose personal habits match their professional accomplishments. It's one of the most important concepts I've learned in all of my life.

The truth is you don't break a bad habit; you replace it with a good one.

Listening without bias or distraction is the greatest value you can pay another person.

Chapter 10

Empowering Others:
The Secret to Winning Relationships

LEADING BY INSPIRATION

A good way to think of leadership is the process of freeing your team members to do the best work they possibly can. Today's business team members say they want, more than anything else, the autonomy to do their jobs without the boss's interference. It's already clear that the CEOs of our best-run companies believe that the more power leaders have, the less they should use. The job of the team leader is to set a mission, decide upon a strategic direction, achieve the necessary cooperation, delegate authority—and then let people innovate.

The key to authentic leadership is to listen to your followers, and then open the door for them to lead themselves. The secret is empowerment. The main incentive is caring and recognition. The best leaders today lead by inspiration, not intimidation.

Show a genuine interest in your team members' personal goals and interests, as well as their professional performance evaluations. Convince them by your actions that you have their successes in mind, not just your own agenda. Keep your promises. All true loyalties and long-term relationships are based on mutual trust.

Power and sharing are polarized concepts. Sharing exposes us to considering the needs of others, thus subordinating some of our own desires for gratification. The power habit is fueled by ego and status symbols. Power is like drinking saltwater. The more you drink, the thirstier you get. The thirst and drive for power are everywhere, but they are especially present in the corporate and business world. Until recently, the command and control style of top-down leadership was in style. Leaders demanded respect, rather than earning it. I remember one Fortune 500 CEO who had monthly meetings of all his division managers, conducted around a giant conference table equipped with microphones, and capable of seating 150 people. Division managers had to make their reports and be subjected to his ruthless interrogation. He seemed to delight in tearing a weak presentation to shreds, and more than one manager was reduced to tears under the grueling pressure. His intimidating style worked for a while; however, he ended up being ousted by shareholders as revenues and profits sank over time. He had created soldiers who only complied to orders, but were unwilling or afraid to risk, create, or innovate, because of the fear of upsetting the boss.

The greatest communication skill of all is in paying value to others. That means really listening to others, asking questions, drawing the other person out, asking for examples, asking them to put it in other words, and feeding back for clarity and understanding. This skill of paying value to others, or creating other winners, is called the "I'll make them glad they talked with me" attitude. This great idea is so simple, it's almost deceptive. We have to examine it carefully to understand how it works and why.

The "I'll make them glad they talked with me" attitude is one that can become a whole way of life. When successful individuals face a member of their family, a potential friend, a prospect, or an adversary, or when they pick up the telephone, their attitude is service-oriented, not self-oriented. Their concern is for the other person, not just themselves. When we have someone else's interests at heart, not just our own, other people can sense it. They may not be able to put into words why they feel that way, but they do. On the other hand, people get an uneasy feeling when they talk with a person who has only his or her own interests in mind and not theirs. There is an excellent reason why we all get these feelings about these people. It's known as nonverbal communication. It's the old business of "what you are speaks so loudly, I can't hear what you are saying." And it's tremendously important to all of us.

People, whether they know it or not, telegraph their intentions and feelings. Whatever goes on in the inside shows on the outside. We receive most of these nonverbal communications below the conscious level of thinking. Our subconscious level of thinking evaluates them and serves them up to us as feelings based on past experience. When we adopt the "I'll make them glad they talked with me" attitude, the idea of helping others solve their problems, we have their interests at heart. Then the feelings they receive agree with what they hear us say and the climate is right for both of us to benefit. Everybody wins with this attitude.

The greatest leader and communicator I have ever met was the principal of my children's grammar school, Dr. Roger Rowe. It is the only K-8 school I know where neither kids nor parents look forward to graduation. His approach is legendary throughout California, maybe even throughout the country. His stated philosophy of education is: "To be aware of the uniqueness of each individual and to treat that uniqueness with loving concern. To provide each student with the opportunities appropriate to his or her abilities and interests. To encourage each one to develop an 'I can, I will' attitude. To help kids go a step above and beyond what they themselves or even others expect of them, and not be surprised when they do."

He knew, by name, every student he ever supervised or taught over his 30-year career. He communicated on a first-name basis with every student and parent. He knew how individual fifth graders scored on their math tests today and how all the second graders did in their poem project yesterday. He called monthly to congratulate us on our children's progress. His office was open to students and parents alike. The results speak for themselves. Good scholarship and citizenship have abounded, and behavior problems, as well as the incidence of drug abuse, have been almost non-existent. And before they graduate from the eighth grade, nearly all the kids are able to pass the same test required of high-school seniors.

Roger Rowe is the master example of the "I'll make them glad they talked with me" attitude—the idea of helping other people solve their problems by having their interests at heart. His case history has been implemented within many different types of organizations ranging from sports franchises to financial institutions, and from small entrepreneurial start-ups to major retail and service corporations.

Because our world is changing so rapidly, particularly in areas of social networking, our IQ, or mental intelligence, is not enough to help us live a successful and fulfilling life. We must learn to develop our EQ or EI—emotional intelligence, which is the ability to understand and monitor our own feelings, as well as those of others.

The five most important words a leader can speak are: "I am proud of you."

The four most important are: "What is your opinion?"

The three most important are: "If you please."

The two most important are: "Thank you."

And the most important single word of all is: "You!"

To motivate individuals over an extended period of time, it is important to understand the psychology of human motivation. Basically, motivation can be external or internal, as we have discussed before. External motivation pulls you forward by some tangible reward you'll attain by taking action. Internal motivation means doing something because it inspires your own sense of inner self-worth and contribution to society. While both are important to achievement, intrinsic or internal motivation creates long-term commitment and loyalty more than simply the promise of external rewards. There are, of course, many successful entrepreneurs who are more "money motivated" than in changing the world. There are equally as many successful entrepreneurs who are predominantly interested in improving the quality of life for others and who reap great financial rewards as a by-product of this vision of service.

We all want financial security. We all want to determine our own destinies. Most of us are motivated by material or external accomplishments to measure our success. However, money alone, generally, will not sustain loyalty or motivation. There is a plateau or "burn out" point when money no longer motivates, because a certain comfort level has been reached. Loyalty requires an inner force that compels commitment after standard of living needs have been met. Far too many people have disconnected their personal mission in life from their business or profession.

The primary step in promoting loyalty is helping others define and pursue their own "magnificent obsessions." A magnificent obsession is the way you want to live, not just the things you want to own. It is the person you want to be, not just the title you want after your name on your business card. A magnificent obsession is the mindset that you have, not the degrees you earn. It is the worldview that you claim as your own, not the collection of stamps in your passport or photos in an album. Your magnificent obsession will cover all areas of your life including how you want to live, to think, to work, to play, to grow, to create, to worship, and to spend your precious hours, days, and years on this earth.

Questions: If it weren't for money, time, and personal responsibilities, what would you really love to do with your life? What do you really get excited about? Five years from now, what will your days be like? What will you be doing? Where will your focus be professionally? How will you be spending your time? With whom will you be spending your time?

Great leaders create loyalty by aligning their own visions for the future with the specific life goals of their followers. This does not mean convincing others to follow the leader's vision. It does mean helping others define and reach their own, individual magnificent obsessions via the same vehicle or business plan.

Actions: Show a genuine interest in your team members' personal goals and interests, as well as their professional performance evaluations. Convince them by your actions that you have their interests and successes in mind, not your own selfish motives which you are accomplishing through them. Keep your promises. All true loyalties and long-term relationships are based on mutual trust. Break the trust and you break the relationship. Integrity is the cement that solidifies loyalty, no matter what obstacles occur along the way.

LISTENING: THE LOST ART

Empowered teams require a new communication style. In the old, traditional work group, you want compliance. In an empowered team, you want initiative. Directional communication (announcing decisions, issuing orders) inhibits team input. If the team leader or supervisor is still using "boss" language, the team gets the message that they're being told what to do.

Managers of empowered teams need to learn to ask open-ended questions and develop the skill of truly listening to the answers. Listening is a lost art, which must be rediscovered. Few people really listen to others, usually because they're too busy thinking about what they want to say next. In business transactions, clear communication is often colored by power plays, one-upmanship, and attempts to impress rather than to express. In our work, as well as our personal lives, how we listen is at least as important as how we talk. Genuine listening to what others want would allow more sales to be made, more deals to be closed, and greater productivity to be gained. Although it's not always necessary or possible to satisfy those wants, understanding them is the glue of a relationship.

Not paying value by listening is a way of saying, "You're not important to me." The results are reduced productivity (I don't count here, so why should I even try?), employee turnover (Who wants to work in a place where I don't feel valued?), absenteeism (I'm just a cog in the wheel, only noticed when I make a mistake), retaliation (They only listen when the griping 's loud enough), lost sales (They don't seem to understand I need), and dangling deals (I can't get through to them; 'alking to a brick wall). Genuine listening can cure a range of supposedly intractable problems.

stion: Are you able to listen openly to others, without judgment?

Actions: Even if you have excellent presentation skills and have an authoritative and persuasive ability to speak to those you lead, make a conscious effort to convert your team meetings into creative dialogue where you ask open-ended questions and solicit feedback and input from all those present. Everyone can be a source of useful ideas. The people closest to the problem usually have the best ideas. Learning flows up as well as down in the organization. Nothing is sacred except the governing vision and values. The process of open dialogue improves performance. The more information people can access, the better.

Most importantly, don't view any suggestion or comment from the group as inane, silly, or irrelevant. Appearing foolish in front of one's peers is a major embarrassment and stifles any future desires to offer ideas that might be considered "off the wall." The most common mistake in communicating is saying what you want to say, rather than what they need to hear and then listening to what they have to offer. It's rightly been said that you can get more people to vote for you in twenty minutes by showing interest in them than you can in twenty weeks by showing how interesting you are.

When you think back in your life to the people you love and respect most, they have been the ones who have been there for you, in person, day in and day out, no matter what. By actually considering your team as your own "performance review" scorekeepers, you will spend the time and effort required to earn their respect by respecting them and keeping them informed of both the good and bad news ahead for the organization. Often those lowest on the pay or hierarchy scale are closest to the customer and therefore most aware of problems in delivering quality goods and services as advertised. Having an active suggestion system in place that pays attention to and rewards innovation in making the organization more effective and efficient is crucial to success in a volatile, competitive economy.

One of the most revered and respected motion-picture actors, whose personal life matched the inspiring roles in all of his movies, James Stewart, was asked his definition of leadership. Always unassuming, unimpressed with his fame, and humble, he answered:

"What is a leader?

"Real leaders come in all shapes and sizes, genders, ethnicities, religions, cultures, beliefs, and from all walks of life. But they all have a few things in common:

"They are never so big that they can't bend down to help someone else.

"They are never so wise that they don't remember who taught them.

"They are never so gifted that they won't share their skills with others.

"They are never so fearless that they don't play by the rules and live by the law.

"And they are never such big winners, that they forget what it feels like to lose."

Impostors, who want power over others, try to convince their employees, teammates, subjects, fans, students, and children to respect and honor them. Authentic leaders work to encourage and empower others to think more of themselves.

It seems so simple, doesn't it? Executives and managers want the respect of their employees—but what they should want is for their employees to respect themselves. Parents want the love and admiration of their children. What they should want is for their children to feel good about who they are and confident about what they can do.

It's never easy to be one of the newest members of a team, company, or even a family. Feeling like a fifth wheel is always uncomfortable. As a leader, be more inclusive than feeling exclusive because of your position. Welcome someone who feels estranged, accept the differences in those who work and live nearby, and see the other person's point of view before passing judgment.

Instead of a numbers game, business today is truly a "motivate the team" game. In a global marketplace where the playing field is anything but level and where there is no job security because of slimmer profit margins due to outsourcing of manufacturing and service functions, it is imperative to maximize the return on investment in the "human capital" already on your payroll. Here are nine steps to empowering team members:

1. Document their accomplishments so they can't pretend they don't exist. Never allow team members to lose sight of their accomplishments, and with it their potential for success.

2. Show them how to find opportunity in adversity. Every outcome, no matter how negative, presents options that were not previously available.

3. Assign them tasks that will display their talents. By transferring important responsibilities to

team members, you demonstrate your confidence in them and give them the chance to succeed in increasingly challenging assignments.

4. Teach them how to get what they want from other people. Teach your people to be assertive rather than too aggressive or too passive.

5. Show them the awesome power of listening, an active strategy for achieving personal success. When your subordinates become better listeners and begin reaping the benefits, they will feel better about themselves.

6. Tell them exactly what you expect of them and find out what they expect of you. The reason most subordinates and team members give for not satisfying their management is not knowing what management expects.

7. Criticize performance but not people. The spirit of criticism should be, "I don't like what you did in this case, but I do like you."

8. Praise not only them but also their performance. You don't want merely to keep your people happy; you want them to know what they did right so they can repeat it.

9. Keep them in ongoing training programs. This gives them a vote of confidence, and carefully chosen training will further contribute to their effectiveness.

As accomplishments mount, self-confidence and ability grow in other areas as well. The more we accomplish, the larger our view of our enormous capacity for creative growth. It has been said that there are no business problems that aren't really "people" problems that impact business decisions and outcomes. Solicit feedback from the bottom up, rather than make edicts and policies from the top down. Total success is the continuing involvement in the pursuit of a worthy ideal which is being realized for the benefit of others, rather than at their expense. And success is the process of learning and sharing and growing.

WALKING IN ANOTHER'S MOCCASINS

A mother had taken her five-year-old son shopping at a large department store during the Christmas season. She knew it would be fun for him to see all the decorations, window displays, toys, and Santa Claus. As she dragged him by the hand, twice as fast as his little legs could move, he began to fuss and cry, clinging to his mother's coat. "Good heavens, what on earth is the matter with you?" she scolded impatiently. "I brought you with me to get in the Christmas spirit. Santa doesn't bring toys to little crybabies!" His fussing continued as she tried to find some bargains during the last-minute rush on December 23. "I'm not going to take you shopping with me, ever again, if you don't stop that whimpering," she admonished. "Oh well, maybe it's because your shoes are untied and you are tripping over your own laces," she said, kneeling down in the aisle to tie his shoes.

As she knelt down beside him, she happened to look up. For the first time, she viewed a large department store through the eyes of her five-year-old. From that position there were no baubles, bangles, beads, presents, gaily decorated display tables, or animated toys. All that could be seen was a maze of corridors too high to see above, full of giant stovepipe legs and huge posteriors. These mountainous strangers, with feet as big as skateboards, were pushing and shoving, bumping and thumping, rushing and crushing. Rather than fun, the scene looked absolutely terrifying! She elected to take her child home and vowed to herself never to impose her version of a good time on him again.

On their way out of the store, the mother noticed Santa Claus seated in a pavilion decorated like the North Pole. She knew that letting her little boy meet Santa Claus in person would go a long way toward his remembering the Christmas shopping disaster as a pleasant rather than unpleasant experience. "Go stand in line with the other children, and sit up on Santa's lap," she coaxed. "Tell him what you want for Christmas, and smile while you're talking so I can take your picture for our Facebook family album."

Even though a Santa Claus was standing outside the store entrance ringing a bell, and although they had seen another Santa at the previous shopping center, the five-year-old was pushed forward to enjoy a personal chat with the "real one." When the strange-looking man with the beard, glasses, and red suit stuffed with pillows hoisted the boy up onto his lap, he laughed loudly (which he felt was important to the role) and tickled the little boy in the ribs. "And what would you like for

Christmas, son?" Santa boomed jovially. "I'd like to get down," the boy replied softly.

Santa Claus was a stranger to the little boy. This youngster was confused by seeing two other Santas before his mother had asked him to get up on the "real" one's lap. It isn't fun for a five-year-old to do last-minute shopping in a crowded mall jammed with impatient adults. By kneeling down and tying her son's shoe, and by considering his uneasiness with a strange Santa Claus, the mother was experiencing a rare lesson in empathy that too few of us ever share with those we care about most. That story made me think of the old Sioux Indian Prayer I have on my desk. It reads: "Oh Great Spirit, grant me the wisdom to walk in another's moccasins before I criticize or pass judgment."

In many small group discussions throughout my career, we have agreed that in communication there is nothing as important as "walking in another's moccasins" before you speak your mind. Empathy is one of the keys to communication. It is "feeling with" the other person. More than sympathy, or "feeling for" an individual, empathy is the process of trying to understand the other person's point of view, as if you were that person. Empathy is when you watch the marathon runners at the 20-mile mark, and your own legs ache. Empathy is understanding what it feels like to be bullied by classmates in school or on the Internet. Empathy is feeling the apprehension or eager anticipation of a newly arrived immigrant to a strange, new country.

Questions: To this day, I often ask myself some questions and try to visualize the answers. How would I like a parent like me, if I were my children? How would I like to be married to me? How would I like a manager like me? These are difficult questions.

Do I only give lip service to being a good communicator? I ask myself. Do I take my relationships for granted or do I truly know what the others in my life are feeling, needing, wanting, and saying?

Actions: Develop that magic touch. Reach out today and tonight and tomorrow and every day for the rest of your life and give someone the value of your attention. Remember, a touch is worth a thousand words or text messages. Text messages are the most impersonal forms of communication. Your personal, physical presence, being there with your employees, being there with your loved ones. The most important motivational message in the world is: I'm here for you because I care for you. You're worth my full attention right now. Being there in person to encourage and support others is the ultimate expression of empowerment.

Here are a few more actions steps to better communication:

It is never too late to communicate. Don't wait for fear of what the response might be. Remember Parkinson's latest law: "The vacuum created by a failure to communicate will quickly be filled with rumor, misrepresentation, drivel, and poison."

In the communication process, knowledge is not always wisdom; sensitivity is not always accuracy; sympathy is not always understanding. Empathy is never assuming anything until you have "walked a mile in another's moccasins."

Look at yourself through other people's eyes. Imagine being your parents. Imagine being that person married to you. Imagine being your child or your employee. When you come into a room or office, what do you think a stranger's first impression will be of you? Why?

View everything you hear with open-minded examination. Be open-minded enough to consider it without prejudice, and be analytical enough to research and test its integrity.

Take full responsibility for success in the communication process. As a listener, take full responsibility for hearing what the others are trying to say. As a talker, take full responsibility for being certain they understand what you are saying. Never meet anyone halfway in your relationships. Always give 100 percent.

And, finally, if you are a parent or plan to be a parent, I offer you my humble rhyme about listening: Take a moment to listen today, to what your children are trying to say. Listen today, whatever you do, or they won't be there to listen to you. Listen to their problems, listen to their needs. Praise their smallest triumphs, praise their simplest deeds. Tolerate their chatter, find out what's the matter. Amplify their laughter, find out what they're after. But tell them that you love them every day and night, and though you scold them, make sure you hold them, and tell them things will work out right. Take a moment to listen today to what your children are trying to say. Listen today, whatever you do, and they will come back to listen to you.

No gift can ever replace the value of being there in person.

_____

Always give more in valuable service than you expect to receive in payment.

Chapter 11

"Servant Leadership":
Looking Beyond "Me" and "Selfies"

THE WIN-WIN LEADER IN
A WIN-LOSE WORLD

Winning has a new definition for individuals and organizations as we speed through the decades of this 21st century. It used to mean beating the others and being Number One at any cost. Winning signified standing victoriously over a fallen adversary—"the survival of the fittest." Remember the slick TV commercial that tried to convince us that: "You don't win silver, you lose gold"? The "Win-Lose" philosophy that suggests that there must be a loser for every winner, that winning by intimidation is fashionable, is obsolete.

Instead of "I win—you lose," the new definition must be, "Let's win together!" The real winners in the present and future world arena will be more often the champions of "cooperation" rather than merely "competition." The "Win-Win" philosophy is the only one that can endure. "Win-Win" means: "If I help you win, then I win too!" True winners get what they want by helping others get what they want. Independence has been replaced by interdependence. There are too many people, too few resources, and too delicate a balance between nature and technology to produce winners in isolation today. We are interdependent in terms of security and survival. We have the capacity to thrive together or perish together. We must face the inescapable fact that we as individuals are a vital but single organ of a larger body of human beings in the world. The one cannot succeed, or even survive for long anymore, without the others. Instant access to information erases all boundaries, except those that are cemented in our minds.

Win-Win appears simple on the surface. Read a self-help book or two; attend some "mindfulness" and "emotional intelligence" workshops; learn about the qualities of a win-win person; do a little role-playing, and then go out and succeed. After all, what's so hard about applying, "If I help the other person win, I win, too"? Actually, quite a bit. Before we can successfully practice "win-win" precepts, we have to recognize three major hurdles that stand in our way:

1. The win-lose philosophy is natural.
2. The win-lose philosophy is dominant in our society.
3. The win-lose philosophy is habit-forming and addicting.

We live in a culture that is basically dedicated to the win-lose philosophy. It's a point of view that has become natural for us. No one blames you for "looking out for Number One" as long as you are discreet and law-abiding about it. Some adults live their entire lives at an emotional level that ranges from childlike to adolescent. The chief symptom? Preoccupation with the immediate gratification of self and its senses. The child's rationale is an uninhibited, "If it feels good, do it!" The adolescent approach climbs a bit higher on the ladder to say: "If it feels good, do it, as long as you don't hurt anybody else." This adolescent rationale is held by many adults who go their win-lose way "doing what comes naturally." The admission that win-lose living is natural doesn't mean that it is healthy, or that it will help society thrive and endure in the long run. Earthquakes, floods, anger, violence, and the "fight or flight" response are also natural though not necessarily healthy phenomena. Some tip-offs that reveal the win-lose approach include:

- Caring for others only to the extent that those others provide you with self-gratification ("What can she do for me?")

- Enjoying relationships only so long as they do not compromise selfish needs ("I'll love you if or when...")

- Withdrawing into materialism, the possession of things, which creates the fantasy of success in a vain hope to banish frustration and emptiness ("Yes, I paid a bundle for it, but it's only money.")

- Wanting to pay as little as possible for pleasure and fulfillment ("There must be a free ride in this somewhere.")

The win-win lifestyle is the antithesis of the above. In fact, about a decade ago, evolutionary biologists and psychologists began finding neural and possible genetic predispositions to cooperation rather than selfishness. The win-win person is prepared to pay the price of some self-deprivation in the cause of caring for others. No one is capable of giving love unconditionally all the time, because the natural win-lose (look out for Number One) attitude is always in the way. But an encouraging sign of true maturity and love is that you're increasingly willing to devote more time and effort to caring for others than trying to satisfy your own real or imagined needs. This is the win-win philosophy, and it often doesn't come naturally!

Authentic winners are those individuals who in a very natural, free-flowing way seem to consistently get what they want from life by providing valuable service to others. They put themselves together across the board—in their personal, professional, and community lives. They set and achieve goals that benefit others as well as themselves. You don't have to get lucky to win at life, nor do you have to knock other people down or gain at the expense of others.

Winning is taking the talent or potential you were born with, and have since developed, and using it fully toward a purpose that makes you feel worthwhile according to your own internal standards. Happiness, then, is the natural by-product of living a worthwhile life. Happiness is the natural experience of winning your own self-respect, as well as the respect of others. As we said in an earlier message, you can't buy it, wear it, drive it, swallow it, inject it, or travel to it! Happiness is the journey, not the destination.

spend your life learning, exploring, growing, losing, ning, and, if you are unselfish, trying to make a positive contribution. Your life is a collection of moments and memories. It also is the legacy you pass on to family and future leaders. The lessons you leave in your own next generation—as core values—are far more priceless than the material valuables you will leave them in your estate. Life is governed by universal laws that have remained unchanged since the beginning of recorded time. Actions cause reactions. Rights carry responsibilities. Truth promotes trust. Thoughts become things. Love is to life as the sun is to planet Earth. Every choice carries a reward or consequence. In the long run, like rings within a tree, each of us becomes the sum total of our actions.

With respect to authentic happiness and quality of life, there are pros and cons with our ever-evolving cyber life. Our reality is becoming more virtual by the minute, and there are signs that we are developing into a new culture of "moist robots." Moist, in the sense that we still are fleshy, warm-blooded, emotional humans. Robots, however, as we become one with our smart devices and artificially intelligent and stimulating virtual environments.

As I travel globally, I see the smartphone selfie as the preoccupation of most tourists, obsessed with providing Facebook, Instagram, or texting proof that they were at this special place. Being in the photo, to many, is more significant than the joy and deep emotion of the majesty, awe, and beauty of the experience itself. In defense of the digital age, I marvel at the benefits that technology offers to stay connected with those far away, to expand our knowledge exponentially, and to enhance the quality of life for hundreds of millions of people worldwide.

However, as you experience the wonders of life on earth in person, inhale all the sights, smells, music, tastes, textures, and cultures that you possibly can. Take your gaze off the screen in the palm of your hand, relax your fingers on the miniature text keyboard, and stare at the big picture of your surroundings, rather than size up your photo op through the tiny window on your cell phone camera. Make sure you live in the moment, rather than back home with the stored images of the memory.

There are pros and cons concerning our preoccupation with cyber-life. To a certain extent, technology is the enemy of intimacy in that smiley-faced texts often replace face-to-face interaction. Cell phone selfies appear to be a method of capturing special moments to relish and share on Facebook. However, I have noticed something unsettling about the tourists on my safaris to observe the wonders of nature in Alaska, the Serengeti in East Africa, the South Sea Islands, the Galapagos, and other historical sites. Many of the tourists are so obsessed with selfies to show others back home that they were at this special place, they miss the essence of the big picture—the overwhelming beauty, majesty, and awe of that once in a lifetime, incredible, sensory moment. Being in the photo, to many, is more significant than the joy and deep emotion evoked by the experience itself.

In defense of the digital age, our virtual work lives, and our geographically challenged personal relationships, technology helps us stay connected with loved ones and friends, work teams, peers, and colleagues who we otherwise would not have an opportunity to see face to face.

Questions: As you check off the items on your "bucket list," be mindful of not simply what you can take home as a pleasant memory. What did you learn from the environment and the culture? How did it make you better and wiser? Did it make you more grateful for what you have?

Actions: Think about what you can give back to the experience. On a recent trip to Malawi in Africa, one of my guides admonished me for giving young children two of my unused bottles of drinking water. "It will only quench their thirst for one day," I was reminded. I returned the following summer and financed a well to serve the small village we had visited. It was the very least I could do.

We've made a little list of things we'll do more and less of from now on:

Laugh at our misfortunes more and at other people's predicaments less. Spend more time counting blessings, less time scrutinizing blemishes.

Spend more time playing with children and grandchildren, less time watching professional athletes perform. More time enjoying what we have, less time thinking about the things we don't have.

Walk in the rain more without an umbrella and listen less to weather reports. Spend much more time outdoors in New Zealand and East Africa and much less time in tall buildings and big cities.

Eat more of everything healthy and delicious, less of everything each meal, saving enough on the bill to feed a starving child.

Do more listening and less talking so we can learn to understand rather than being desperate to be heard. Spend more time looking at trees and climbing them, less time flipping through magazines made from dead trees.

Get more beach sand between our toes and less friction between ourselves and others. Take more long baths and fewer showers.

Spend more time with old people and animals, less time with strangers at clubs and parties.

Act the age of children and grandchildren more and act our own ages less. Give our loved ones more tender touches and much less advice.

Spend more time fully involved in the present moment, less time remembering and anticipating.

Become more aware of our core values and life mission, and less concerned with the reasons why we might not measure up.

Smile more, frown less. Express feelings more, try less to impress friends and neighbors.

Forgive and ask forgiveness more and curse our adversaries less—but most of all we'll be more spontaneous and active, less hesitant and fearful.

When a great idea or spur-of-the-moment adventure pops up—a safari of any kind, an open house at school, a game of hide-and-seek, an opportunity to solve a problem at work or to satisfy a disgruntled customer, to understand someone who looks and believes differently than we do, to go on a hayride, to be invited to build a snowman or paint over graffiti, to watch a lunar eclipse or a double rainbow—we'll be more inclined to jump up and say, "Yes, let's do it!"

We're going to dedicate ourselves to live this new way every day. We'll never have all the moments we've missed, but we do have all the time remaining.

THE ROAD BEST TRAVELED

In our life's journey, we must remember that success is a process, not a destination, let alone a summit. The road best traveled was inspired by "The Road Not Taken," a well-known poem by Robert Frost. To visualize the road best traveled, you must understand that it's not what you have that counts—not your money, stocks, IRAs, gold coins, silver bars, cars, position, or real estate. What counts is what you now do with what you have. No one can reasonably claim that the choices are easy. I trust I'll never forget M. Scott Peck's great book, *The Road Less Traveled*, whose opening line consists of three words: "Life is difficult."

No doubt it has always been difficult in various ways, but some stretches are more difficult than others, and the world has known far easier, happier periods. In some respects, the planet is spinning out of control. The increase of crime, especially violent crime, is frightening, not only in itself but also for what it says about the underpinnings of our family life, our sense of responsibility, our cultures. Many of our children seem destined to live in a world of angry anarchy, with all that means for society as a whole. As we've seen, the middle class must struggle harder and harder to earn its living—whose standard is declining. We worry about our children, in this respect and others. Confusion grows, tempers are raw, relationships are strained, the traditional human optimism has been worn thin. Economic security—security of every kind—seems to be disappearing. All of this is true, and most of it is rightfully worrying—but at the same time, the opportunities for personal growth and success are unparalleled.

Our society's current condition reminds me of another first line, this one by Charles Dickens. The famous "It was the best of times, it was the worst of times," which opens *A Tale of Two Cities*, could easily serve to summarize our own times. It is the worst of times as measured by some aspects of our global life, especially in the demoralized, decaying, and impoverished regions. But age brings perspective, and perspective can offer the refreshing appreciation that things are not quite as bleak as they appear. This is not the first appearance of "the worst of times," throughout the world. The way out is through personal commitment to individual and collective goals—yours and mine.

As we grow older, we recognize that certain battles are no longer worth fighting. Therefore we choose our conflicts carefully, just as we choose the road on which we walk with increasing care. Which road is best? As Robert Frost said, t road less traveled made all the difference. If that's the you've chosen—never mind whether you're racing ahead, struggling on an upgrade, or resting a moment while you catch your breath—you know that life is not a book that is finished when you've read its last pages. You know that it is more like a garden that changes with the seasons. It grows well in the summer and less well in the fall. What you planted in the spring might die in the winter. But when you plant again, tending the soil and watering the seeds, you will reap again. You also know that it's not necessary to invite weeds into your garden. They move right in, and in great numbers. No planting is necessary but getting a life garden to produce flowers of kindness, food for flourishing friendships and success, takes constant attention and vigilance. It demands commitment to the road best traveled.

During many periods of history, farmers left a corner of their crops unharvested so that the less fortunate might use them for food. This ensured that everyone had enough to eat, and also demonstrated the farmers' compassion. It showed that they cared about others and didn't have to have it all in order to feel successful. It was what one did on the road best traveled.

Be a taker and you may even climb to the top of the win-lose heap. You may gain prestige and esteem; you may become powerful and confident; you may even reach what you believe is your "full potential." But inside you most likely will be asking yourself a few big questions:

Questions: Do you consider the quality of the journey as important as the result? Is your definition of success a million dollars or more in your bank account and a vault stuffed with certificates, or is success taking the high road and placing value on people—your family and others whose goals you can help reach?

If you could balance the demands of your business and personal life with more outside activities, what would you choose? To spend some weekly time reading to the elderly in a community retirement home? Take more walks on the beach or in a park? Volunteer for a drug awareness program for teenagers?

Why did I spend my life climbing to the top, while not enjoying the view or reaching down to lift up others who were reaching up?

Why do I feel lonely now that I have reached the peak?

"In renunciation, it is not the comforts, luxuries, and pleasures to give up," said Mahatma Gandhi. "Many could forgo having meals, a full wardrobe, a fine house, etc. It is the ego that they cannot forgo, the self that is wrapped, suffocated in material things—which include social position, popularity, and power. It is the only self they know, and they will not abandon it for an illusory new self which they may never obtain."

Actions: Travelers on the road best traveled are generous to others because they have a strong sense of their own self-worth. They can give freely of themselves without feeling depleted. They know the only thing they can really keep is what they're willing to give away. These travelers also know that they can never be certain of what lies around the next bend. So they walk in quiet faith, one step at a time, one day at a time, reaching out to one person at a time—starting with their families, then extending to friends, neighbors, and finally to the world at large.

LOVE RETURNS WHEN SET FREE

Just as organizational leaders must learn to empower team members, so must each of us, on a personal level, understand the importance of being a win-win leader with our romantic and life partners. True maturity and love is that you're increasingly willing to devote more time and effort to caring for others than trying to satisfy your own real or imagined needs. The concern about having others serve our needs is how many relationships are perceived, pursued, and destroyed.

True love is an expression of the value we place on a person independent of his or her ability to meet our needs. Authentic love makes you want to set your partner free, not possess him or her. In my own relationships, I like to think I'm more liberating than possessive, that I'm rarely captured by envy or jealousy, that I tend to give without worrying about what I might get in return. But I'm as far from perfect as everyone else.

Sometimes I sense that my tendency to be a good Samaritan nurturer comes from a need for approval. Trying to share my values out of love is one thing. Seeking approbation in order to neutralize the fear of abandonment that may have sprung from my childhood in a broken home is another—and I can't always be certain of my ultimate motive.

How about you?

Question: Do you help others so they can fly free or in hope that they'll approve of you?

Of course, human motives are almost always mixed, but the constant is that the best way to ensure you are loved by those important to you is to empower them to become as independent and valuable as they can be.

Actions: It is better to endeavor to be loveable than desperate to be loved. When others sense that you have their interests rather than only your own at heart, they begin to trust you. That foundation of all friendships and healthy marriages is also the key to customer service and satisfaction. You never just close a sale. What you do is open a long-term relationship based on mutual disclosure and mutual trust.

When we apply the concept of Servant Leadership to raising children, we need to differentiate between being leaders and role models, and not simply servants and ATMs for our children. Childhood should be the time for shifting from primary selfishness to sharing, for learning to cope with deprivation and disappointment—and learning to overcome failure, since breaking a toy and forgetting a homework assignment are far less serious than breaking a marriage or forgetting to prepare for career advancement. But excessive deprivation, as is common in underprivileged families, leaves many children stuck in the stage of personal gratification.

They lack resources for developing a sense of responsibility for others and a wish to care for them. And children needn't be poor to be underprivileged. The overindulged are also deprived, cheated out of learning how to cope. Ironically, it can be more difficult for the wealthy to be effective parents. Children of lower-income families are often forced to learn competence and the need to provide for themselves. Rich parents can easily be tempted to use money or things as bribes to gain affection or establish control. Their children, in turn, sense that the mom and dad who can no longer do without their high standard of living are weak parents. It takes strength and discipline for the privileged to stop manipulating and being manipulated.

One of the media's more destructive myths is glorification of the child-centered home. Rather than revolving around children, the home should be based on the loving commitment of adults whose relationship provides a model. Child-centered homes promote selfishness and an unnaturally elevated sense of importance on the part of the little princes and princesses, retarding development of open, loving relationships.

The more we do for our children after the age when they're capable, the less they can do for themselves. The less they do for themselves, the more we rob them of the opportunity to gain self-respect. Without self-respect, the deprived ego begs for approval and attention. Attempting to blame others for our troubles, trying to manipulate others to get what we want, we become dependent on others and often resort to violence in a vain attempt to solve our problems and relieve our frustration. Attacking those who disagree with their beliefs, the selfish and insecure try to prove they're right with might.

Have-nots release their resentment by attacking the haves, demanding their fair share. Haves exhibit disdain of the have-nots who can't control their rage. This vicious, no-win cycle will continue until human beings, who must have a sense of consideration and responsibility for others' well-being, stop shouting and start listening.

Your children will develop the capacity for independent love in place of dependent need only when you set them free to become adults. And only when you set your romantic and business partners free to be all they can be will you know how attractive and lovable you are yourself, free of the insecurity and self-doubt that spawn envy and jealousy.

Commitment to a single partner offers the greatest potential for a win-win life. It combines the natural selfishness of wanting another person to fulfill longed-for fantasies with the chance to be your vulnerable self, able to reveal your innermost thoughts. Just as it takes effort to nurture children to become independent and to empower employees to assume responsibility, it takes real effort to bolster your commitment to your life partner. Healthy love can't be demanded or taken for granted. It can only be a continuing give-and-take exchange and dialogue between two independent persons who share many values and responsibilities, yet still feel a childlike magic with each other. That's the deepest message of this chapter: Love returns when it is set free.

Here are some tips for healthy personal relationships and raising win-win children:

1. Look at yourself through others' eyes. Imagine being married to you. Imagine being your child or your friend.

2. Check to see if you shift roles easily and appropriately from worker/executive and earner to

nurturing parent, and from role model to romantic partner.

3. Listen unconditionally to the significant adults and children in your life. Listening without bias or distraction is the greatest value you can pay another person.

4. Develop a magic touch. Don't assume that money, shelter, and creature comforts are enough to demonstrate your love. Nothing can replace your presence, your hug, your touch—you.

5. Be aware of opportunities to add spice and romance to your most important adult relationship: flowers, a greeting card slipped into a briefcase, an unexpected phone call, an overnight bag in the car trunk when it was supposed to be just dinner and a movie.

6. Talk casually and evenly with your children, not as an authority figure. Parents under stress often withdraw from one another and from their children, communicating in a terse, irritated way. To ensure that your children feel accepted, take time to chat with them about anything and everything, a message that says, "I'm interested in you."

7. Become enthusiastic about your family members' interests. Young children need their parents' involvement and approval—but remember that involvement shouldn't mean taking over or becoming their agent and manager.

8. Schedule mandatory family time together, even at the expense of seemingly pressing obligations. Family members often meet coming and going, making the home like a pit stop at the Indianapolis 500. One meal a day together with the television off is a bare minimum.

9. Except where safety may be involved, give your family members the responsibility for the consequences and rewards of their own choices. Don't take over when that will rob them of the experience of the independent action that develops self-trust.

10. Build a home atmosphere in which each family member respects the needs, dignity, and individuality of all the others. Make your cornerstones love, caring, trust, and giving.

11. Maintain an atmosphere that encourages free and open communications. Encourage all family members to express feelings and opinions without fear of recrimination or reprisal.

12. Above all, encourage every family member always to take the high road of being a caregiver rather than the low road of being a share-taker from others. Although not most traveled, the high road is always the road best traveled.

Love is one of the few experiences in life that we can best keep by giving it away.

Time is an equal opportunity employer. Each human being, while living, has exactly the same number of hours and minutes every day. Rich people can't buy more hours. Scientists can't invent new minutes. And you can't save time to spend it on another day. Even so, time is amazingly fair and forgiving. No matter how much time you've wasted in the past, you still have an entire today.

Chapter 12

"Walking the Talk":
Being a Role Model Worth Emulating

THE FUTURE IS IN YOUR HANDS

We live in a fast-forward world with more changes in one of our days than in a decade or more of our grandparents' lives. You are at the center of what is being transformed into the greatest economic and geopolitical power base for the foreseeable future. This metamorphosis is one of the most awesome examples of human ingenuity and perseverance in recorded history. You have both the opportunity and responsibility to create a harvest of abundance and fulfillment for yourself and your inner circle. Each of us must be willing to stand out while fitting into our organizations and society. We must be team leaders, not just team members. We can no longer say: "Why don't they do something?" We must say, instead: "Here's what I am doing to solve the problem, by thinking globally and acting locally."

There's a Chinese fable about a wise man who lived outside a large village. Every Saturday he would come into the main square, and the villagers would surround him to be healed or to gain words of wisdom, which the wise man had been doing for years. There also lived nearby a young, self-centered man who was jealous of the wise one and resented his popularity. The young man had a plan to embarrass the wise man. His scheme was to come into the village square with a dove tucked inside his hands and ask the old man if he knew what was in his hands. If the old man guessed correctly, he would ask another question, "Is the dove alive or dead?" If the wise one said it was alive the young man would push his hands together and break the dove's neck. If the wise man said it was dead he would simply open his hands and allow the dove to fly into the sky. In either case, he would prove the old man wrong.

So with his plan in place, the young man set off toward the village square in the mid-afternoon at the busiest time of day. As he approached the old man, the wise one was busy helping people with different problems and offering words of wisdom. The young man confronted the wise one and speaking loudly, so everyone could hear, he said: "Hey, old man, I have a question for you." The wise man turned and smiled: "Yes, of course, what is it?" The crowd, sensing something of a showdown, moved in closer. The young man continued: "My question to you is what do I hold in my hands?" The wise one smiled and said, "Well that's easy. You have a beautiful dove in your hands." The young man chuckled, "Well, can you tell me if it is dead or alive? The wise man paused, reflected, yet hesitated to answer.

The young man, relishing his apparent checkmate, retorted: "Well old man, you seem to be at a loss for words." The villagers were silent with anticipation, as tension filled the hot afternoon air. The young man, sensing victory, shouted: "For years and years you've had an answer for everything! What about now old man? What about now?" With this last statement the wise man gave his trademark smile and replied in his steady, friendly manner: "Young man, the fate of that lovely dove is in your hands."

So it is with change in your life—it's up to you. There are only two choices facing leaders today and in the future: You must become change masters or become obsolete as change victims. Today, in the knowledge-based world, where change is the rule, a set of personal strategies is essential to success, even survival. Never again will you be able to go to your place of business on autopilot, comfortable and secure that the organization will provide for and look after you.

In order to gain the respect of others, we must first earn it. We must be respectable. In order to be a role model, we must first set a positive example. In order to lead others, we must first lead ourselves. You must look in the mirror when you ask who is responsible for your success or failure. You must become a lifelong learner and leader, for to be a follower is to fall hopelessly behind the pace of progress.

What worked yesterday won't work today. Why? Yesterday natural resources defined power. Today knowledge is power. Yesterday leaders commanded and controlled. Today leaders empower and coach. Yesterday leaders demanded respect. Today leaders earn respect and encourage self-respect. Yesterday employees took orders. Today teams make decisions. Yesterday value was extra. Today value is everything. Yesterday profits were earned through expediency. Today profits are earned with integrity. Yesterday what you learned in school was sufficient. Today learning is lifelong.

The secret to enjoying the greatest benefits of life is to smell the roses through the journey and not wait for the destination. The consensus is that the two great tragedies in life are never to have had a great dream to strive for and never to have fully reached it. You see, happiness seems to be associated more with the daily experience of the journey than the fleeting moment of the recognition of having arrived. Success, then, is the process of learning, sharing, growing, and welcoming change.

MISSION IN REVIEW

Our mission in this book has been to help you empower yourself and those who look to you for leadership to be inspired to embrace excellence as authentic champions in the game of life. In Chapter 1, we encouraged you to look at yourself from the inside, assessing your own unique talents and skills, seeking out the best in your field and putting those examples to work for you. You found that what stands in the way of reaching your greatest aspirations is past conditioning and psychological limitations, rather than physical limits. You realize that your self-image is like a thermostat that you can reset for peak performance.

Chapter 2 dealt with one of the most important concepts of all—internal values. The value-centered give of themselves freely and graciously, constantly seeking to bring out the best in others.

Open and modest, they have no need for conceit, the opposite of core value. Feeling good about who they are, and not needing to constantly talk about their victories or line their walls with associations with celebrities or their awards, people with core values spend much of their time "paying value" to others.

Chapter 3 discussed one of the most difficult human qualities to attain, which is non-situational integrity. All relationships are based on mutual trust. Break that trust and you break the relationship. Creating a long-term relationship takes two or more people—whether executives, representatives of labor and management, or couples who are grounded in and operating on the same non-situational integrity.

Chapter 4 featured cause and effect and the realization that winners make it happen and losers let it happen. Taking personal responsibility for the outcomes in our life means that we live by choice, not by chance, and exercise our free wills to control our destinies.

Chapter 5 helped you face your fears and focused on dwelling on the rewards of success, not the penalties of failure. Motivation is best when the desired result is your motive in action. You can't concentrate on the reverse of an idea.

Chapter 6 reaffirmed the inextricable relationship between our minds and bodies, and that optimism is the biology of hope. Faith and belief are among our greatest powers for success and good health. Expectation is an unfailing boomerang bolstered by the Law of Attraction.

Chapter 7 taught that your mind stores as reality what you vividly, repeatedly imagine. A mantra you heard throughout this program is: "What you visualize and internalize, you can come to realize and materialize." We believe Einstein was right. Imagination is more important than knowledge, for knowledge is limited to all we now know and understand, while imagination embraces the entire world, and all there ever will be to know and understand.

Chapter 8 urged you to set meaningful goals important to your career and personal life. A goal is a dream with a deadline and should be specific, measurable, achievable, really yours, and time based, if it is a material achievement. All you need now is to think of your brain as a target-seeking GPS system that can be rewired to create a freeway to your destination. Tell your mind where you are and where you want to go, and it will take you there.

Chapter 9 was all about the development of healthy habits and the incredible power of the mind to make winning a reflex by observation, imitation, and repetition. Self-discipline is doing within while you are doing without, and it shows us how to practice winning images, thoughts, and emotions to create permanent success. Neuroscience now confirms that new neural pathways in the brain are created by guided imagery.

Chapter 10 concentrated on empowering others. Leadership is the process of freeing your team members to do the best work they possibly can. Today's business team members say they want, more than anything else, the autonomy to do their jobs without the boss's interference. Empowered teams require a new communication style. In the old, traditional work group, you want compliance. In an empowered team, you want initiative.

The best leaders and managers in the world look for value and pay value often to members of their team. Their motto is: If you win then I win too.

In the previous Chapter 11, we spoke in depth about the double win in action. We showed why being a servant leader is the key to synergy and success in today's turbulent marketplace, where change is the rule. We pointed out that a shared vision and a shared harvest are fundamental qualities in an authentic leader and champion. While "selfies" feature us, being unselfish and having a cause that benefits others is the road best traveled.

In this 12th and final chapter, I have saved my most critical message for last. Of all the wisdom I have gained, the most important is the knowledge that time and health are two precious assets that we rarely recognize or appreciate until they have been depleted. As with health, time is the raw material of life. You can use it wisely, waste it, or even kill it. To accomplish all we are capable of, we would need a hundred lifetimes. If we had forever there would be no need to set goals, plan effectively, or set priorities. Yet in reality, we're given only this one life span on earth to do our earthly best. Each human being now living has exactly 168 hours per week. Scientists can't invent new minutes, and even the super-rich can't buy more hours.

We worry about things we want to do—but can't—instead of doing the things we can do—but don't. How often have you said to yourself, "Where did the day go? I accomplished nothing," or "I can't even remember what I did yesterday." That time is gone, and you never get it back.

Staring at the compelling distractions on a television screen or your computer, tablet, or smartphone screen is one of the major consumers of time. You can enjoy and benefit from the very best it has to offer in about seven total hours of viewing per week. The irony is that the entertainers and athletes we are watching are having fun achieving their own goals, making money, having us look at them enjoying their careers.

Even so, time is amazingly fair and forgiving. No matter how much time you've wasted in the past, you still have an entire today.

FREEDOM FROM URGENCY

Time management contains one great paradox: No one has enough time, and yet everyone while living has all there is. Time is not the problem; the problem is separating the urgent from the important. Every decision we make has an "opportunity cost." Every decision forfeits all other opportunities we had before we made it. We can't be two places at the same time. Even though we all are aware of the tradeoffs of "quality time vs. quantity time" in our relationships, we are not used to thinking specifically about how our decisions cost us other opportunities. Without this understanding, our decisions will often be unfocused and unrelated to helping us achieve our most important goals. To live a full, balanced life we need to be more in conscious control of our habits and lifestyles.

Freedom from urgency—that's what will allow us to live a rich and rewarding life. You may have thought your problem was "time starvation," when in truth, it was in the way you assigned priorities in your decision-making process. Have you allowed the urgent to crowd out the important? Each day we will continue to encounter deadlines we must meet and "fires," not necessarily of our own making, we must put out. Endless urgent details will always beg for attention, time, and energy. What we seldom realize is that the really important things in our life don't make such strict demands on us, and therefore we usually assign them a lower priority. The local university doesn't call us to advance our education and improve our life skills. I have never received a call or e-mail from the health club I joined insisting that I show up and work out for thirty minutes each day. My bathroom scale has never insisted that I lose thirty pounds. Nor have I ever been subpoenaed by the ocean or the mountains to appear for relaxation and solitude. Yet I receive hundreds of urgent phone messages, texts, and e-mails each week from people with deadlines. You see, it's the easiest thing in the world to neglect the important and give in to the urgent. One of the greatest skills you can ever develop in your life is not only to tell the two apart, but to be able to assign the correct amount of time to each.

Beginning tomorrow, throughout the day, and every day thereafter, stop and ask yourself this question: "Is what I'm doing right now important to my health, well-being, and mission in life, and for my loved ones?" Your affirmative answer will free you forever from the tyranny of the urgent. And most importantly, your loved ones, especially your children, will place more value on the time you spent with them than they ever will on the money you spent on them and the valuables you left them in your estate. Take time to hear a robin's song each morning. Take time to smell the roses as you go. Before you leave, please say "I love you" to the ones you know. Take time out for a sunset and its afterglow. Take time to climb a tree with kids this summer. Explore each country back road you can find. And take a moment now and then to build a castle in the sand. Take time to hike that mountain when you can. Take time to play; your work can live without you. Give up the urgent for the afternoon. And take a loved one by the hand, and slowly gaze at that full moon. Don't let this minute pass you, for the years go by too soon. Take time today, to share and give, before it slips away. Take time to live.

How do you measure success? For me, success and winning are very personal. They mean something different to each of us. For me, it's not what you get that makes you successful, it is what you are continuing to do with what you've got. Happiness and fulfillment seem to be associated with the richness of the experience in the journey, not in the fleeting moment of recognition of having arrived. You can't gain success and then sit back and enjoy it like a giant lollipop that never melts away. This is why some of the superficial self-help myths leave us empty and hungry for the truth. Success is not a destination; it is a way to travel. A feeling of inner joy and success seems much harder to acquire than a Mercedes, a stallion, or a castle with a wine cellar.

To feel successful deep inside, we need to understand why we were created, who we are, and what we really want in life. One wealthy, happy, and successful entrepreneur confided, "I could have made a lot more money in my life, but I preferred to sleep well at night." This individual found the ideal combination: outer as well as inner success, but only because of the realization that all success must be built from the inside out.

As I have learned through my own wins and losses, the success of others has little to do with my personal success. True success is not measured by what others may say or accomplish. Though we all tend to compare ourselves with others, the happiest people in life know that they don't really compete against others. Their success comes from doing their best, based on their passion and inner motivation. Instead of achieving or performing to impress the world or your peers, seek to do something that is beautiful, excellent, and heartwarming. Suppose, for example, you set out to learn to play a certain piece on the piano. You practice hard and long on the difficult concerto, and then you play it. You may play the piece one day for an audience of one or many, but that isn't why you seek to master it. You do it for the sheer exhilaration of doing your best. You need no one else to measure you or your skill. Your gallery is your private relationship with your Creator and your own self-respect.

Real success comes in small portions day by day: a smile, a hug, a sunrise or sunset, beach sand between your toes, a satisfied customer, a child's happy squeal, the smell of lilacs, a hand extended, a phone call from a friend, a tree, a tasty meal eaten without haste. The list is endless, but our minutes to enjoy and appreciate life's small successes are not. If there is one thing I want my children and grandchildren to learn from me, it is to take pleasure in life's daily little treasures. It is one of the most important things I have discovered about winning and measuring success.

In these chapters, I have tried to distill the essence of what I have been seeking to communicate for the past five decades, plus timely tips based on benchmarking champions in every field. Victory is not gained only at someone's expense. Every victory does not result in a defeat. Being the best is identifying the talent or potential you were born with and using it as fully as possible toward a purpose that makes you feel worthwhile and at the same time benefits others.

Success is not a matter of simply gaining financial wealth. I believe we all should seek financial security; in fact, it ensures that our golden years can be spent with freedom of choice and dignity. But money is like a plane ticket. It will take you nowhere unless you use it. A ticket does you no good if it is preserved and worshipped for its own sake. Actually, money and knowledge are very much the same. They mean nothing when you simply collect them. They mean everything when you employ them, share them, and put them to work.

I believe there is a way to be happy and contented. I believe we can master the skills, attitudes, and disciplines needed to be the best we can be. I believe there are keys that unlock the door to all our dreams of satisfaction and happiness. We can be whole persons who function more completely, effectively, purposefully, and gracefully. And when we can do that, we will understand success and winning the game of life.

When I was very young, I dreamed I could do anything, be anything, have everything. I wished upon a star and saw myself go everywhere throughout the world, without a care. But somehow in between I asked myself: Could it be? Should I see? All this for me? And now at last I know, what kept my sights too low were simply childhood fears I learned so long ago.

How do we know that the vision we see for ourselves is real? How does that face in your mirror reflect how you truly feel? When do our doubts and our fears disappear? When do we know that the harvest is near? Who can we turn to? Who do we trust? To lift us up year after year? So many questions searching for answers. So many voices from youth. So many hours of working and waiting. Then, finally, a moment of truth. The secret to unleash the champion inside you is really quite simple to find. Give all your attention to the visions before you. Leave all of your failures behind. Cherish the loved ones around you. Stay true to the friendships you share. Let health and abundance surround you. Dream as big as you possibly dare.

Imagine that all you desire and hold dear is asking permission from you to appear. This is your moment. This is your year. Don't wait for the future—it's already here.

End

Winning for Life:
Making Every Day, Rich in Every Way

SYNOPSIS FOR YOUR SMARTPHONE

In the event that you want to revisit the key points covered in this book in a convenient way, here are the key elements of all 12 chapters that you can photograph and review on your tablet or smartphone and/or share with your colleagues and family.

1. If you can see something in your mind's eye, and you imagine it over and over again, you will begin to believe it is really there in substance. As a result, your actions, both physical and mental, will move to bring about in reality the image you are visualizing. We encouraged you to look at yourself from the inside, assessing your own unique talents and skills, seeking out the best in your field and putting those examples to work for you. You found that what stands in the way of you reaching your greatest aspirations is past conditioning, which creates invisible barriers. These are psychological limitations, rather than physical limits. You now realize that your self-image is like

a thermostat that you can reset for peak performance. What you set is what you get.

2. Healthy self-esteem is perhaps the most important and basic quality of a winning human being. You want to be able to say, "I like myself. Given my parents and my background, I'm glad I'm me. I realize I may not be the best-looking in the group, but I always look my best in every group. I'd rather be me than anyone else in the world." This is the self-talk of a winner. Winners have developed a strong sense of self-worth, regardless of their status. They weren't necessarily born with these good feelings, but they've learned to like themselves through practice. The value-centered give of themselves freely and graciously, constantly seeking to bring out the best in others. Open and modest, they have no need for conceit, the opposite of core value. Feeling good about who they are, and not needing to constantly talk about their victories or line their walls with associations with celebrities or their awards, people with core values spend much of their time "paying value" to others.

3. Non-situational integrity is one of the most challenging qualities to attain. All relationships are based on mutual trust. Break that trust and you break the relationship. Creating a long-term relationship takes two or more people—whether executives, representatives of labor and management, or couples who are grounded in and operating on the same non-situational integrity. When *Fortune* magazine asked the CEOs of many Fortune 500 companies what they considered the most important qualities for hiring and promoting top executives, the unanimous consensus was that integrity and trustworthiness were by

far the key qualities. That survey of leading businessmen—not of preachers or motivational speakers—speaks for itself.

4. Winners take full responsibility for determining their actions in their own lives. They believe in cause and effect and have the philosophy that life is a "do-it-to-yourself" program. People who are aware that they exert control over what happens to them in life are happier and are able to choose more appropriate responses to whatever occurs. All individuals are what they are and where they are as a composite result of all their own doings. Although our innate characteristics and environment are given to us initially, the decisions we make determine whether we win or lose our particular game of life. My friend and colleague, the late Stephen Covey, defined responsibility in his own way: "Look at the word *responsibility* as two words: response and ability—the ability to choose your response," wrote Stephen in his best-selling *The Seven Habits of Highly Effective People*. "Highly proactive people recognize and embrace responsibility. They do not blame circumstances, conditions, or conditioning for their behavior. Their behavior is a product of their own conscious choice based on values, rather than a product of their conditions, based on feeling."

5. Desire motivation is the inner drive that keeps you moving forward in pursuit of your goals. Winners in every field in the game of life are driven by desire. There never has been a consistent winner in any profession who didn't have that burning desire to win internalized. The success of our efforts depends not so much on the efforts themselves, but rather on our motive for doing them. The greatest companies and the greatest men and women in all walks of life have achieved their greatness out

of a desire to express something within themselves that had to be expressed, a desire to solve a problem using their skills as best they could. Whatever you do, never allow your goals and their benefits to you to get lost in the back of your subconscious. Bring them out in the sunlight and shine them every day—and there's no way you can fail. A fear is a goal in reverse. Dwell on the problem and it grows. Dwell on finding a solution and the mind moves toward that dominant thought. Losers dwell on the penalties of failure. Winners dwell on the rewards of success. Your expectation is what drives your motivation.

6. Faith and belief are among our greatest powers for success and good health. Expectation is an unfailing boomerang bolstered by the Law of Attraction. Research done by the Yale School of Public Health and the National Institute on Aging found that young people who had positive perceptions about aging were less likely to have a heart attack or stroke when they grew older. And another study confirmed that middle-aged and elderly people lived an average of seven years longer if they had a positive perception of aging. Faith and belief are among our greatest powers for success and good health. Expectation is an unfailing boomerang bolstered by the Law of Attraction. How does your lifestyle—your expectations and your forecasting—affect your own health and well-being? Optimism is an incurable condition in the person with faith. Optimists believe that most disease, distress, dysfunction, and disturbance can be remedied. Optimists also are prevention and wellness oriented. Their thoughts and actions are focused on solutions, health, and success. They concentrate on positive outcomes and rewards, rather than the penalties of failure. What the mind harbors,

the body manifests. You may not get what you want in life, but generally speaking, you are much more likely to get what you expect.

7. We believe Einstein was right. Imagination is more important than knowledge, for knowledge is limited to all we now know and understand, while imagination embraces the entire world, and all there ever will be to know and understand.

We all have fantasized and acted out our "life scripts" at some point in our lives. The mind can't distinguish between imagined and real experience. The mind stores as truth everything vividly rehearsed and practiced—which is why it's so vital to store winning instead of losing images. And to correct your mistakes as they are made, focusing on how to do it right next time. This is the centerpiece of our program. A mantra you heard throughout this program is: "What you visualize and internalize, you can come to realize and materialize." To your brain, a dress rehearsal is the opening night performance. Getting in touch with your five senses will greatly enhance your ability to layer new, positive habits over the old ones. Your imagination has the incredible ability to pre-play and replay sensory events as if they were really happening at the present moment. This is testimony to the universal truth that thoughts become things. Imagination plus repetition creates internalization and, ultimately, realization.

8. Dream big, with laser focus. When goals are kept in focus and are approached in orderly progression, they ignite the human mind's awesome creativity and powers of accomplishment. Concentrate your attention on where you want to go, not

away from where you don't want to be. You will always move in the direction of your current dominant thoughts. Think of your mind as a marvelous GPS system, but instead of a Global Positioning Satellite system, either handheld or in our cars, your brain is like a GPS system, where GPS means Goal Positioning System. Tell your internal GPS where you want to go. Be as specific as possible. The more inputs the better. And it will guide you there. But first you must know where you are right now. And where you want to go. Ask yourself, "Can this goal be timed, checked, or measured?" If you cannot time, check, or measure your performance, your goals are not specific enough. The mind does not compute ideas like "doing your best," "doing better," "getting rich," "being happy," or "having enough." It deals only with specificity, not vague ideas. What are your income needs for next year? What is your desired weight? What amount of cash asset do you need to save that will give you enough income to enjoy your life in the future, after taxes, without depending upon employment? You have a gold mine, in your goal mind.

9. We learn by observation, imitation, and repetition. We observe role models and others. We imitate their behavior. We repeat that behavior until it is internalized like brushing our teeth or driving our cars. Observation, imitation, repetition, internalization. The force of habit is your greatest tool for success. We all first make our habits; then our habits make us. Habits are like submarines; they run silent and deep. The chains of our habits are usually too small to be recognized until they're too strong to be broken. The secret is repetition, repetition, repetition. Repetition creates habit. Habit becomes conviction. Conviction controls action. What we need most in

life is continuing support and reinforcement of other winners with similar goals. Every week, meet before work, after work, or during lunch with one or more role models. Form a network with other success-conscious associates in your local community. In everything you do, think, speak, act, behave, and get the habit of success by association. Your mind and body can't distinguish rehearsal from the main event. It stores as reality whatever you practice. You become that to which you are most exposed. Constantly expose yourself to successful individuals whose personal habits match their professional accomplishments. It's one of the most important concepts I've learned in all of my life.

10. Leading by inspiration. A good way to think of leadership is the process of freeing your team members to do the best work they possibly can. The job of the team leader is to set a mission, decide upon a strategic direction, achieve the necessary cooperation, delegate authority—and then let people innovate. The key to authentic leadership is to listen to your followers, and then open the door for them to lead themselves. The secret is empowerment. The main incentive is genuine caring and recognition. Even if you have excellent presentation skills and have an authoritative and persuasive ability to speak to those you lead, make a conscious effort to convert your team meetings into creative dialogue where you ask open-ended questions and solicit feedback and input from all those present. Everyone can be a source of useful ideas. The people closest to the problem usually have the best ideas. Learning flows up as well as down in the organization. The most common mistake in communicating is saying what you want to say, rather than

what they need to hear and then listening to what they have to offer. It's rightly been said that you can get more people to vote for you in twenty minutes by showing interest in them than you can in twenty weeks by showing how interesting you are. In many small group discussions throughout my career, we have agreed that in communication there is nothing as important as "walking in another' s moccasins" before you speak your mind. Empathy is one of the keys to communication. It is "feeling with" the other person. More than sympathy, or "feeling for" an individual, empathy is the process of trying to understand the other person's point of view, as if you were that person.

11. Win-win leaders in a win-lose world. Authentic winners are those individuals who in a very natural, free-flowing way seem to consistently get what they want from life by providing valuable service to others. They put themselves together across the board—in their personal, professional, and community lives. They set and achieve goals that benefit others as well as themselves.

Winning is taking the talent or potential you were born with, and have since developed, and using it fully toward a purpose that makes you feel worthwhile according to your own internal standards. Happiness, then, is the natural by-product of living a worthwhile life. Happiness is the experience of winning your own self-respect, as well as the respect of others. You can't buy it, wear it, drive it, swallow it, inject it, or travel to it! Maturity and love mean that you're increasingly willing to devote more time and effort to caring for others than trying to satisfy your own real or imagined needs. The concern about having others serve our needs is how many relationships are perceived, pursued, and destroyed. True love is an expression of the value we place on a person independent of his or her ability to meet our needs. Authentic love makes you want to set your partner free, not possess him or her. It is better to endeavor to be loveable than desperate to be loved. When others sense that you have their interests rather than only your own at heart, they begin to trust you. That foundation of all friendships and healthy marriages is also the key to customer service and satisfaction. You never just close a sale. What you do is open a long-term relationship based on mutual disclosure and mutual trust.

12. Of all the wisdom I have gained, the most important is the knowledge that time and health are two precious assets that we rarely recognize or appreciate until they have been depleted. As with health, time is the raw material of life. You can use it wisely, waste it, or even kill it. To accomplish all we are capable of, we would need a hundred lifetimes. If we had forever, there would be no need to set goals, plan effectively, or set priorities. Yet in reality, we're given only this one life span on earth to do our earthly best. Each human being now living has exactly 168 hours per week. Scientists can't invent new minutes, and even the super-rich can't buy more hours. We worry about things we want to do—but can't—instead of doing the things we can do—but don't. How often have you said to yourself, "Where did the day go? I accomplished nothing," or "I can't even remember what I did yesterday." That time is gone, and you never get it back. Even so, time is amazingly fair and forgiving. No matter how much time you've wasted in the past, you still have an entire today. Real success comes in small portions day by day: a smile, a hug, a sunrise or sunset, beach sand between your

toes, a satisfied customer, a child's happy squeal, the smell of lilacs, a hand extended, a phone call from a friend, a tree, a tasty meal eaten without haste. The list is endless, but our minutes to enjoy and appreciate life's small successes are not. If there is one thing I want my children and grandchildren to learn from me, it is to take pleasure in life's daily little treasures. It is one of the most important things I have discovered about winning and measuring success. Beginning tomorrow, throughout the day, and every day thereafter, stop and ask yourself this question: "Is what I'm doing right now important to my health, well-being and mission in life, and for my loved ones?" Your affirmative answer will free you forever from the tyranny of the urgent. And most importantly, your loved ones, especially your children, will place more value on the time you spent with them than they ever will on the money you spent on them and the valuables you left them in your estate. Live as if each new day were your last, while dreaming and learning as if you were going to live forever.

About Denis Waitley

Best-selling author and speaker, Denis Waitley has painted word pictures of optimism, core values, motivation and resiliency that have become indelible and legendary in their positive impact on society. He has studied and counseled leaders in every field, including Apollo astronauts, heads of state, Fortune 500 top executives, Olympic gold medalists, and students of all ages and cultures.

THANK YOU FOR READING THIS BOOK!

If you found any of the information helpful, please take a few minutes and leave a review on the bookselling platform of your choice.

BONUS GIFT!

Don't forget to sign up to try our newsletter and grab your free personal development ebook here:

soundwisdom.com/classics